Why Do Things
Go Wrong?

For
Father David
whom I have never heard complain
in his long struggle against
cystic fibrosis

Why Do Things Go Wrong?

David Self

A LION BOOK

Published by
Lion Publishing plc
Sandy Lane West, Oxford, England
ISBN 0 7459 3137 5
Albatross Books Pty Ltd
PO Box 320, Sutherland, NSW 2232, Australia
ISBN 0 7324 1270 6

First edition 1995
10 9 8 7 6 5 4 3 2 1 0

Acknowledgments
Bible quotations from the Revised Standard Version
© 1989, by the Division of Christian Education of the
National Council of Churches of Christ in the USA and used
by permission
Bible quotations from the Good News Bible © American
Bible Society, New York, 1966, 1971 and 4th edition 1976,
published by the Bible Societies/HarperCollins, with
permission.
'The Long Silence' pp 85–87 copyright © Fellowship of
Christian Athletes
The author and publishers would like to thank the Dean of
Winchester, the Very Reverend Trevor Beeson; Mr Riadh
El-Droubie; and Mrs Margaret Wymer for permission to
quote their words, and also to thank the Rt Hon the Lord
Jakobovits for permission to quote the late Moshe Davis.
The author would also like to express his gratitude to those
teachers, preachers and writers whom he had heard and read
over the years and who have helped formulate his ideas.
Every effort has been made to trace owners of copyright
material but in some cases this has not proved possible. The
publishers would be glad to hear from any others.

A catalogue record for this book is available
from the British Library

Printed and bound in Great Britain
by Cox & Wyman Ltd, Reading

Contents

Preface

As a boy, Keith had gone to church. He'd even been in the choir for a time while he was at primary school. But he must have stopped going soon after he was twelve or perhaps thirteen.

It was only much later, when he met Christine, that Keith started thinking about church again. Christine was a regular churchgoer, and Keith knew it all meant a lot to her. In fact, he sometimes wondered whether her Christian faith was stronger than her love for him—and his love for her.

From the time they were officially engaged, Keith began going with Christine to church. It was what she so obviously wanted. Gradually, it began to make sense to him. Two years after they were married, he was confirmed. Keith had realized his newfound faith made sense of things, and helped him in all sorts of ways.

A year later, Christine's cancer was diagnosed. She died the day before their fourth wedding anniversary.

As the illness had taken its hold, Keith had felt anger: a savage, black anger at God for allowing it to happen—especially to someone who believed as firmly as Christine did. Why her, of all people? She was *good*. She was one of God's people. It made no sense.

After Christine died, Keith's anger faded, only to be replaced by a mixture of bitterness and confusion. He was bitter that he'd wasted time in 'believing'. He was confused because Christine's faith had so obviously been important to her (he knew she'd prayed twice a day until they started the morphine). So why had it all happened the way it did?

I dare to hope this book may be of some help to Keith—and to those with similar doubts and confusions.

I hope it may help those who find that all the suffering in the world prevents them from believing in God, as well as those who do believe but who are disturbed by doubts when they think or read about suffering, or see its helpless victims on television or in their own lives.

When I was a schoolteacher, the commonest jibe flung at Christianity by both the thoughtless and thoughtful who sat in my religious education classes was this: 'OK, so if there is a loving God, why does he allow all this suffering?'

In 1980, I had a chance to provide a serious answer to that taunt. BBC School Radio invited me to make five programmes for teenagers which looked at ways the different world faiths—Hinduism, Buddhism, Judaism, Islam and Christianity—tried to answer the same question. Later, I made another programme on the same topic for an adult audience. During this time, I interviewed scores of priests, rabbis, monks, teachers, doctors and other people who were coping with different kinds of suffering. To them, I owe a great deal. They provided many wise answers and helped me to sort out my own thoughts.

More recently, over a five-year period, I was able to help care for my mother (a deeply committed Christian) as she suffered terribly and eventually died from a disease of the liver. Despite my clever radio programmes, and just like Keith, night after night I asked God in my prayers, '*Why?*'

Why this suffering? What's it *for?*

This book is my attempt to answer that question. I pray it helps you to sort out *your* answer.

David Self

Introduction

If you don't believe in God, it's easy.

You believe that, in the beginning and quite by chance, there was a big bang. Some sort of primeval atom exploded, creating a huge space filled with a kind of cosmic soup. Gradually, and by accident, lumps of this soup congealed to form galaxies. Somehow or other, these lumps of matter then began to organize themselves into stars and planets.

And again by accident, water began to slosh about on one of these planets and, in that water, blue-green algae began to form. And still by accident, some of this algae changed to form sponges—then jellyfish and worms and reptiles and birds and mammals and humans...

If you believe that the process of evolution (indeed, the whole of creation) was all an accident, then you must believe that things can very well go wrong in an accident-prone universe. In fact, it would be amazing if they didn't. And there would be a lot of suffering. No problem.

If you believe that God *did* create the universe and bring life into being, but then buzzed off somewhere, leaving it all to get on as best it could by itself, then there's still no problem. Things would be bound to go wrong in such a haphazard set-up.

If, moreover, you also believe, as many people have done, that God is either cruel, vengeful or simply absent-minded, then again there is no reason why there shouldn't be suffering in the world.

And if you believe in God but also believe in a devil who is just as powerful as God, there's still no problem. Sometimes God wins and everyone's happy. Sometimes the devil wins, there's hell to pay and everyone's miserable.

What if ...

But suppose you believe:

◆ **There is a God who brought the universe into being (either literally as the Bible tells us or gradually through the process of evolution); and that**

◆ **God is all-powerful; and that**

◆ **God is interested in his creation and cares about it and indeed loves all living things ...**

◆ **... then there is a problem.**

To put it another way: for the non-believer, suffering can be explained away as an inevitable part of an imperfect universe; for the believer, it can't.

11

Real problems

For Christians who believe that God looks after us as an all-powerful, loving father would, then yes, there is a real problem.

A very big problem. If God really is caring and loving, why does he allow things to go wrong? Why does he allow so much wickedness and cruelty? Why so many accidents and disasters?

Why does he let lifeboats sink at sea?

Why did he let Hitler remain in power so long?

Why did he arrange things so that rabbits get eaten by foxes?

Why does he allow cancer cells to grow?

Why doesn't it rain in Africa when it's needed?

And why did God create the world so that there are tidal waves and floods and earthquakes?

Why should he allow suffering?

Not so long ago, there was a ghastly road accident near the village where I used to live. A teenage girl was killed one Saturday night when the car she and her friends were in crashed into a tree. As the police swept up the broken glass on the road, a neighbour said to me, 'Well, it's all God's will.'

That strikes me as a lousy answer. The God I worship couldn't possibly have willed that.

But I *do* believe there is a single God who created the universe. I do believe he is what I'll call 'almighty' (I'll come back to this in Chapter 9), and I do believe he is interested in his creation and continues to care about it, and about us.

And I *don't* believe in letting God off the hook by

saying that suffering is all just part of some divine mystery.

So what is my answer to the question, 'Why is there evil and suffering in the world?'

Well, to save you being disappointed later, let me admit at once that I have no easy answer. It would be amazing if I did have one. Far better minds than mine have tried to answer this question for hundreds, even thousands, of years; and they've not come up with one simple, watertight answer.

But I do have some possible answers—and I don't believe you have to be a masochistic saint who enjoys suffering in order to accept them. Since God has let us invent interior sprung mattresses, I see no need to seek out a bed of nails.

So how are we going to answer the question, 'Why does God allow suffering?'

Pain and suffering

Before we begin, I'd like to point out that in this book I shall be using the word 'pain' to mean a physical sensation—that feeling when part of the body hurts.

'Suffering' I shall use to mean something greater. Suffering can include, or result from, physical pain, but it also includes the agony of wishing things were not as they are.

We 'suffer' when a tragedy happens in our lives; when we experience misery or grief. We 'suffer' when we are rejected or unwanted; lonely or frustrated. We suffer when we are *distressed*.

13

We also suffer when we have to watch someone else in distress, perhaps when we nurse a dying relative or when we watch a report about the victims of war or famine. We suffer just as Jesus did when once he saw Jerusalem and wept for what was to happen.

Three types

There are three more distinctions before we start our search for an answer:

◆ **Suffering can be caused by our own inhumanity. That is, it can result from our deliberate cruelty (in the home, in the school playground—or in a war); from our greed for power or possessions (when a mugger hits an old-aged pensioner—or when one country attacks another); and from our straightforward nastiness.**

◆ **Suffering can be caused by our carelessness and incompetence. We drive when we're drunk; we market a drug before it's been proven to be safe; we build a town exactly where a river is likely to flood.**

◆ **Finally, there is suffering which results from 'natural' disasters such as the typhoon or earthquake, the baby born with a deformity, or the illness with no known cause or cure.**

And, as we may as well be logical, let's start with the first.

1

The Things We Do

It happened in Auschwitz, Sobibor and Treblinka in Poland.

It happened in Belsen, Buchenwald and Dachau in Germany.

In extermination and concentration camps in these places, between 1933 and 1945, more than sixteen million people were killed.

Of these victims, six million were Jewish; ten million were Ukrainian, Polish and Russian. They included civilians and prisoners of war. Hundreds were killed because they were socialists; others because they were homosexual.

Some were starved to death. Some were tortured. Others were killed in 'experiments'. Thousands were executed in gas chambers. Thousands more were hanged or shot.

And all this happened deliberately.

It was no accident.

It was the deliberate intention of Adolf Hitler and his followers.

The Killing Fields

In 1979, 2,000 skeletons were discovered in a lake near the town of Stung Treng in Cambodia. They had been tied together with ropes and weighted with stones before they were drowned. They were just a few of an estimated 1.4 million people who were murdered or starved to death in the period when that country was under the power of the Communist Khmer Rouge régime and its leader, Pol Pot. He was determined to wipe out the middle and educated classes. They (and others) were driven into rural areas and there they were treated ruthlessly. Whole families, villages—even entire tribes—met their deaths on the Killing Fields of Cambodia.

Hutu and Tutsi

On 6 April 1994, a plane carrying the president of the Central African country of Rwanda was shot down. He and the president of neighbouring Burundi, also in the plane, were killed.

No one knows who carried out the attack but, in Rwanda, the majority—the Hutu people—blamed the minority, the Tutsi tribe. Civil war had been smouldering since 1990 and the plane crash fanned the embers. Hutu militias (gangs of killers, trained by the government) immediately set upon the Tutsi people. In the resulting genocide, the bloodshed was horrific. Pregnant women had their babies cut out of their bellies. Rivers were choked with corpses. The

Hutu killers made their way through the country, killing any Tutsi person they could find—and any of their own tribe they suspected of helping or hiding a Tutsi family. In just a few weeks, 500,000 people were butchered in what was supposedly a mainly Christian country.

The will of God?

Three of the worst acts of genocide in the twentieth century. The deliberate, savage and systematic murder of whole peoples. How can such things be the will of God? Especially of a loving God?

The answer is, of course, that such things are *not* the will of God. He does *not* want them to take place. They are the very opposite of what he wants, and he is more distressed by them than we can imagine. Just as Jesus once wept at the thought of how the city of Jerusalem would suffer, so God saw Auschwitz and wept.

But if he doesn't want such things to happen, why *do* they happen?

They happen because we let them.

That is the simple fact. There is no other reason. Such evil is our fault.

Free will

We can choose how we behave. Sometimes we choose to do wonderful, kind, loving things. Sometimes we choose to do the most terrible deeds.

God has given us the freedom to choose: he has given us what is called 'free will'.

So great is his love for us that he has trusted us. He could have made us so that we automatically loved him and did exactly what he wished. Then, of course, there would be no suffering, no misery.

But then our love for him wouldn't be real—because love can't be forced. No one, not even God, can *force* someone to love.

◆ So if we are to be able to love God *genuinely* and to follow in his ways, we must be free to choose whether we love him or not—and, to that end, he has given us free will.

But this isn't quite the same as freedom, or being free.

Born free

Most of us who live in the affluent First World are far richer than those who live in the Third World. Therefore we have more choices open to us—how to spend our time, our money and so on. We have more freedom. Oh yes, I know that the eleven-year-old boy who lives next door to me may feel he isn't all that free—he is made to tidy his bedroom, he has to go to school and he has to help with the washing up. But he has far more choice than the eleven-year-old boy in Thailand who is forced to earn a living as a prostitute.

The mother in Ethiopia who died of famine in front of her children may not have felt she was free at all. Nor, almost certainly, did the soldier in World War I who knew he was likely to be shot if he stayed in the front line but even more likely to be shot if he ran away.

Yet even if circumstances limit our 'freedom', we still have the God-given gift of 'free will'.

This is the freedom to make moral choices. To decide whether it would be better to do one thing or to do another... to do it today or tomorrow... to say what we're thinking or to keep silent...

◆ Do I tell my sister I think she's wearing the most unsuitable clothes for where we're going and risk a row, or do I keep my mouth shut?

◆ Do I write that letter to my bereaved friend in Sydney today, or shall I put it off till tomorrow?

◆ Do I take the exciting new job or, for the sake of the family, stay in the boring, well-paid one?

Condemned to be free

Nowhere else in creation does there seem to be an animal that has such freedom of choice, such free will, as do humans. Animals have instincts. So do we. We know we must eat, sleep and so on. But we are also free to make moral choices like the ones above.

And, most of the time, we want that freedom. We relish being able to make decisions. We'd hate it if we were dictated to every second of the day: what we should do, what we should say, or how we should think. We don't really want to lead a dog's life.

All right, there are times when it might seem nice *not* to have to make up our minds. 'Decisions, decisions, always decisions,' we moan—often when we're tired. As the French writer Jean-Paul Sartre once put it, we feel 'condemned to be free'.

Usually, though, we are more than happy to be free, to have freedom of choice. We don't want to be pre-programmed machines. We are glad to have the gift of free will.

▨▨ God takes a chance

But this free will brings with it the possibility that we may not choose to be kind, caring, merciful and forgiving. We may choose to be vicious, greedy, violent and downright nasty. God has taken that risk. He's given us the choice, and pointed out our responsibilities to one another. A lot of the time we realize this.

◆ For example: you and I both probably realize that, even if we desperately need a bit of cash, it's wrong to hit an old lady on the head and steal her purse.
Unfortunately, not everyone does realize this— and old people get cruelly mugged. And the suffering that results is not the will of God. It is the will of the mugger.

◆ Another example: most nations are happy with their boundaries. They might like more land, but they know the nation next door has a right to its own territory. Occasionally, however, in one country or another, an unsuitable ruler comes to power—and decides he *will* invade a neighbouring state. The result is war and suffering. But nor is that suffering the will of God. It is simply the will of the ruthless invader.

So this is the result: if people are to be free to do good, they must also be free to do wrong. It doesn't mean that God is happy for us to do wrong; simply that he loves us and (amazingly) respects us enough to give us the choice.

Born or bred?

It is at this point that some people start to wonder whether, deep down, we are naturally good, naturally bad, or neither. Put it like this: when we are born

◆ are we innocent, inclined to be loving and good— but sometimes we do wrong, having picked up bad habits from others?

◆ are we naturally evil and have to learn how to be good?

◆ or are we neither good nor bad to start with, but simply the result of how we are brought up?

The novelist William Golding seemed to think the second was the case. In his book, *Lord of the Flies*, he describes a group of schoolboys who are stranded on a desert island. With no adults to keep control, the children rapidly break the rules they have made for themselves; they turn savage and some of them start bullying and even killing the weaker members of the group.

Whether we think evil is born or bred in us, we have to admit that we do possess baser instincts. These surface especially in times of war, as the writer Doris Lessing has pointed out:

> *In times of war, as everyone knows who has lived through one, or talked to soldiers when they are allowing themselves to remember the truth, and not the sentimentalities with which we all shield ourselves from the horrors of which we are capable... in times of war we revert, as a species, to the past, and are permitted to be brutal and cruel.*
>
> *It is for this reason, and of course others, that a great many people enjoy war.*

And when people do begin to enjoy war—well, that can lead to all sorts of hellish things.

The root of all evil

What is for certain is that we are all capable of doing wrong. Every day we are selfish, thoughtless or just plain catty. We know this in our hearts. Christians believe that 'through Jesus Christ' they are forgiven when they own up to their failings, deliberate or accidental—when, as the jargon has it, they 'confess their sins'. Because after confession comes forgiveness from God, through Jesus, and the chance for a new start.

Where it all goes wrong is not when people start thinking they don't need to take stock of their lives and admit what's wrong. It goes wrong when they start to think there's nothing wrong with them in the first place. It can all begin very simply.

'Daddy, Daddy,' said the little boy, 'why did you call Granny a bloody old cow?'

'I'm not having you using language like that. I'm taking you upstairs and I'm going to wash your mouth out with soapy water. That'll teach you!'

And when Daddy does that, refusing to admit he ever swore in the first place—that is how evil can enter the world.

Evil people are the ones who cannot see wickedness in themselves; and as psychologists have frequently pointed out, when people do not see themselves as doing wrong, they often imagine instead that there is evil in others—as the father did in the boy.

Because of this, people are often destructive when they do evil things—since they think they are destroying some form of evil in others. So dedicated to this are they that they never judge themselves. Not for them the self-doubt which makes them wonder whether they are on the right track. They believe themselves to be absolutely right; nothing need be questioned.

So it was with Hitler. Totally convinced of his own rightness and the 'evil' of those he saw as his enemies, he set about achieving what he called 'the final solution': the destruction of a people he could not stand.

So it was with Pol Pot. Convinced of the rightness of his own politics, he set out to break and destroy those who did not fit into his particular communist vision.

And so it was in Rwanda. When the Hutu decided the Tutsi were evil, so convinced were they of the rightness of their thinking that they set about the destruction of the Tutsi.

De-throning God

Rabbi Hugo Gryn is a survivor of Auschwitz. I once heard him say that evil occurs 'when people de-throne God'. Evil also occurs when there is a refusal to acknowledge sinfulness or wrongdoing—and we all have the potential to slip into such a trap. It's not just people like Hitler and Pol Pot who do this. But whenever it happens, a little more suffering comes into the world—just as it did in that boy's bathroom when the soap was rammed into his mouth.

If only . . . !

The cruelties of humankind, therefore, are not God's fault. Just because he has given us free will is no rea-son to blame him for the suffering caused by our misuse of that free will. But ome people will still ask, if evil on a really terrible scale is let loose (as happened with Hitler and with Pol Pot) why can't God intervene 'just this once'? If he's all-powerful, couldn't he have let one of the plots against Hitler's life succeed? Couldn't the brakes on his car have failed? What about a thunderbolt? If only...! God, they will argue, could have stopped so much suffering.

But if God had secretly bumped off Hitler, what should he have done about Mussolini? And should he have let Hiroshima happen? And if he had secretly prevented that, what about the bombing of Dresden or Coventry? Where should he start and stop intervening?

The answer is that God hasn't made a chaotic world. It's an ordered world, ruled by the laws of nature. If a gun shoots straight it always shoots straight. It doesn't matter if it's held by a man protecting his friends from a charging rhino, or by a murderer. Its path obeys a law of nature.

Of course, God could have made the world in such a way that, every time a villain pulled the trigger of a gun, any good person who was in the way of the bullet would be saved. He could have made the world in such a way that, whenever someone stole some money, the victim would find it replaced by an equal amount. But that, of course, would soon cause chaos with the money supply and a nation's finances. And if nothing too serious happened when we pulled the trigger of a gun, we would soon become totally irresponsible. Worse, we would be less than human.

God *could* have created a world without pain or suffering—but that would have meant taking away our freedom. We'd have been little more than robots. No, he's arranged things so that our actions have their consequences. We've been given freedom to do right or wrong—but we have to accept what happens as a result. That is the price of our free will. And so that we know where we are, there are the 'laws of nature'.

What's important is that we are eternally on the watch—to see that evil does not take hold of us, or of those around us. If only we can concentrate on that, we may prevent some of the suffering in the world which is our responsibility.

Of course not all suffering caused by humans happens as a result of their deliberate wrong or evil actions. But that topic belongs to the next chapter.

▓▓ Summing up . . .

A lot of the evil and consequent suffering in the world is our own deliberate fault. God has given us free will—the freedom to choose how we behave—and we often choose to abuse that freedom.

2

Accidents Will Happen

It was a gloomy Friday morning in October 1966—
21 October, to be precise. It had been raining heavily
in the Welsh valleys and a huge man-made tip of slur-
ry and other waste from one of the nearby coal-mines
began to move. Gathering momentum, it advanced on
the village school, a farm and a row of houses in the
village of Aberfan, near Merthyr Tydfil. The moving
slag-heap, a great black avalanche, engulfed the primary school, killing 116 children and 28 adults.

The deputy headteacher, Mr Beynon, was found
clutching five small children in his arms. All were
dead. Rescuers worked through the day and night,
using their bare hands, to search for possible
survivors. As the Secretary of State for Wales was to
say later, 'A generation of children has been wiped out
of the village.'

Some days later, eighty-two of the children were
buried in a mass funeral.

It also emerged that, back in 1964, a local councillor
(Mrs Gwyneth Williams), had warned Merthyr Tydfil

Borough Council's planning committee that if the tip moved 'it could threaten the whole school'. She asked that the body responsible for the tip, the National Coal Board, should carry out an investigation into the tip's condition. The committee refused her request.

Debris from the colliery was still being dumped on the tip when it began to move.

A full-scale inquiry was held and, the next year, the Aberfan Disaster Inquiry blamed the National Coal Board.

How could it happen?

It was a ghastly event. Those killed must have suffered terribly, if fairly briefly. The parents who had to watch the rescue operation from the school gates must have suffered even more—and suffered for years after. How *could* it have happened?

Unlike the atrocities mentioned in the last chapter (the Holocaust, the Killing Fields of Cambodia, the massacres of Rwanda), the disaster in Aberfan did not occur because of some evil, deliberate action. It happened 'by accident'.

'Accident', of course, seems a pathetically trivial word to describe such a tragedy, but that is what it was: something that no one meant to happen; something that no one, certainly not God, wanted to happen. In fact, it was something that could have been prevented. If the planning committee had listened to Mrs Williams (she died before the tragedy occurred), it might not have happened. If the

National Coal Board had used all the geological knowledge that was available at the time, it might not have happened.

But, as we saw in the last chapter, God has made the world to operate by the laws of nature. If a gun shoots straight, it shoots straight—no matter who's in the way. And if you put an unstable, soggy slag heap on a hill above a village school, it may begin to slip—whether there's anyone in the school or not. We know what's likely to happen. It's not God's fault. We've got free will: the freedom to choose whether we use our intelligence or not. And that means constant vigilance.

God's fault?

Imagine a built-up area: the road isn't particularly busy or dangerous. It has a 30 m.p.h. speed limit. A car is being driven carefully along it at less than thirty miles an hour.

Suddenly, a toddler on the pavement drops a ball he's playing with; it bounces into the road and the little boy scuttles after it. He dies from head and stomach injuries.

Who is to blame then?

Well, without detailed evidence, we can't be sure. Let's suppose the child was too young to be responsible. And let's suppose the driver was sober and careful, slowing down as soon as she saw the child on the pavement. She did everything she could to prevent the tragedy.

So that leaves whoever was supposed to be in charge of the child (or whoever should have taught him his kerb drill). But suppose that person was a caring, loving mother who just for a moment had let her child move outside her grasp. Can she be blamed for that second's lapse? Doesn't it really mean it's God's fault?

In any case, how can he allow such an accident (for that is what it was)? After all, didn't Jesus especially love children? Yes, he did, and of course the last thing God wants is for little children to be knocked down by motor cars, however carefully they're being driven.

But again we come back to the laws of nature. Motor cars are made of metal. They can hurt. We have that knowledge—and the responsibility to see that cars don't come into contact with children too young to understand the dangers. We can't have the gifts of free will and intelligence to make such things as motor cars without the responsibility of controlling them properly.

If we had one without the other, it would mean that no moment's carelessness could ever result in any suffering.

Anyone driving carelessly and hitting a cyclist would leave her uninjured! Anyone leaning too far out of a tower block window would just drift gently to the ground!

It sounds lovely—but think a little further.

◆ It would be a world in which there was no need for
   us to look after each other.

30

◆ It would be a world in which there was no need to do things for the public good.

◆ It would be a world in which there was no need for unselfishness.

◆ There would be no need for us to concentrate, to persevere—or to try to do anything well.

◆ There would, in fact, be no need for us to care for each other; no need even to love one another.

◆ It would be a world without danger.

We'd be little more than protected marshmallows—never getting hurt, never needing to do anything, never needing to try...

After a railway accident in 1927, Sir Herbert Walker (the director of the railway company responsible) said very wisely, 'Accidents do not happen by accident.' Every accident has a cause!

Use your intelligence!

All right, so we've got to use our intelligence: to try to make sure accidents don't happen—that coalmines are safe, that ships don't put to sea when they aren't seaworthy, that bridges are built to the highest standards, that dams won't burst and flood populated valleys...

And we've also got to use our intelligence to

prevent other sorts of accidents: wife-battering, child abuse, family breakdowns, homelessness, unemployment, poverty... the list could go on. I know that 'accident' seems a pathetic, even cruel, word to use to describe such tragedies. But they do often happen by accident. The pressures of modern life mean that, without any deliberately evil intent, a man may lose his temper to such an extent that he ill-treats his wife or lashes out at his children; the unemployment rate begins to rise not out of any evil scheming by one particular government but because of an economic accident—and so on.

And, in most cases, if only we'd been concentrating, and caring, the accident could have been avoided. To put it quite bluntly, if the government gets something wrong and people suffer, it's not God's fault. It's either an incompetent government's fault—or our own fault for electing its members.

▓ Accidental accidents

But what about those accidents that we haven't got the wit to prevent? I don't mean the sort of accident that's caused by the machines we make or by our thoughtlessness, but an 'accident' such as illness? Surely God could have arranged things so that we wouldn't catch measles, chicken pox and mumps? Surely he could stop us having ulcers, flu or cancer?

Some of these questions belong in the next chapter, for they relate to suffering from causes over which we seem to have no control. For the moment, it's important to remember that much illness is our own fault.

God made grapes; we've used our God-given intelligence to make grape-juice into wine. According to the Bible, Jesus once turned water into wine at a wedding feast—and on a really grand scale: 600 litres of it. So there's nothing wrong with wine. But when I drink too much of it, I can still become stroppy, give myself a hangover and even rot my liver. That's not God's fault for making the stuff too strong. The abuse is mine. I should remember how much is enough!

It's also our fault if we, in the affluent First World, eat too rich a diet, make ourselves obese and eventually give ourselves heart attacks. There are enough warnings against gluttony and they go back centuries. It's not just in the last few years that we've learned the benefits of a high-fibre, low-fat diet. The foods that were readily, naturally available in the past were the ones that are best for us. God's not to blame for the excesses of modern business-account lunches.

But what about those things we have only just realized are harmful, such as knowing that smoking causes cancer? It's certainly our fault if we persist in smoking nowadays when there's a warning on every packet of cigarettes and there's so much health education. But what about the people who died before the connection between smoking and cancer was properly understood?

One answer is that, with tobacco, the first warning came pretty early on. It's generally agreed that smoking was made popular in Britain by Sir Walter Raleigh and others around 1585. Only twenty years later, no less a person than King James I was issuing a stern warning:

Herein is not only a great vanity, but a great contempt of God's good gifts, that the sweetness of a man's breath, being a good gift of God, should be corrupted by this stinking smoke.

The King went on to warn of the dangers of passive smoking (when a husband smokes in the presence of 'his delicate, wholesome and clean complexioned wife') and comes very close to medical truth in his final description of the habit:

A custom loathsome to the eye, hateful to the nose, harmful to the brain, dangerous to the lungs, and in the black stinking fume thereof nearest resembling the horrible Stygian smoke of the pit that is bottomless [hell].

King James' statement became widely known—and was then ignored. Whose fault was that? Who was to blame?

Danger: use with care!

The fact is that not everything in creation is harmless. Deadly nightshade, foxgloves, hemlock, laburnum seeds, mistletoe... they're all poisonous, though some can be (carefully) used in medicines—and that's something that has been known since Roman times at least.

In this matter, as in others, we've been given *knowledge*—and it's our responsibility to remember it and to use it well. When we do, so much suffering can be avoided. It's not God's fault.

(Though I don't half wish our knowledge included a cure for the common cold!)

Summing up ...

A lot of suffering in the world is due to our carelessness, incompetence, greed or thoughtlessness. The world God has put us in has its own laws of nature, and he has given us intelligence so we can predict how our actions will turn out. Even so, we let carelessness, incompetence, greed and thoughtlessness cause accidents and suffering.

3

Big Questions

This is where we get to the difficult bit.

But first, we'd better remind ourselves just how far we've got.

A lot of the evil and consequent suffering in the world is our own deliberate fault. God has given us free will—the freedom to choose how we behave—and we often choose to abuse that freedom. Sometimes we do so on a small scale; other times our wrongdoing is far more serious. But it's our fault.

A lot of other suffering in the world is due to our carelessness, incompetence, greed or thoughtlessness. God has put us in a world that has its own laws of nature, and he has given us intelligence so we know how our actions will turn out. We know that carelessness, incompetence, greed and thoughtlessness can cause accidents and suffering. Again, it's our fault.

Yes, I know this still leaves plenty of questions:

◆ Why doesn't a loving God intervene when we're being really stupid?

◆ Surely God can override the laws of nature when he wants?

◆ Does this mean there's no point praying that evil dictators won't come to power and that we won't have accidents?

And so the questions continue. We'll come back to these later on. Honestly. In Chapter 10.

■ 'Natural' disasters

But now, what about the third type of suffering: suffering for which we really can't be blamed? What about the so-called 'natural disasters'?

Take the Algerian earthquakes of 1980. Two big earthquakes almost totally destroyed the North African town of El Asnam. Two housing developments, the main hospital, a large department store and the central mosque were all destroyed. The earthquake measured 7.3 on the Richter scale and was the most violent ever in that part of the world. Government officials reported that 20,000 people died. What's more, it was the second time El Asnam had been hit by an earthquake.

In 1954, 1,600 people had been killed. Lessons were learned then and the city market was rebuilt with foundations designed to withstand future shocks. But they were not good enough. The market was destroyed again (with many resulting deaths) in 1980.

There have been far more lethal earthquakes this century. In 1908, Messina in Sicily was the epicentre of a major quake. In that disaster, some 200,000 people were killed, both by falling buildings and by the tidal wave that followed. In 1923, Tokyo and Yokohama in Japan were struck. 300,000 people died. Around the world earthquakes happen: in San Francisco, Skopje, Nicaragua, Mexico (10,000 lives lost in ten minutes), Guatemala, Turkey, Kobe...

We know nowadays what causes them. Most occur along fault lines (or breaks) in the Earth's crust. There is a build-up of stress as two of the rock-masses or plates that form the Earth's surface slowly move against one another. When they spring free, tension is released in the form of a quake.

Modern scientific knowledge *may* one day allow us to predict earthquakes accurately. In the distant future, technology may even allow us to prevent them by injecting vast amounts of water into the fault lines—but that may be just a dream.

For the moment, they are uncontrollable and cause appalling suffering. As the German writer, Goethe, said after the 1755 Lisbon earthquake which killed 30,000 people, 'Where is God and what is he doing?'

Why indeed does God let earthquakes happen? Surely he's not saying:

◆ Don't live anywhere on the earth likely to have an earthquake

or:

◆ You'll just have to put up with earthquakes until you've learned to use your wits either to build earthquake-proof buildings or to predict them accurately!

If God is 'almighty' (yes, that word again), couldn't he have made the Earth's crust in such a way that its plates don't rub against each other? Just as I keep wondering why aeronautical engineers don't make whole aircraft out of whatever the stuff is they use to make those 'black boxes' that survive crashes, so I wonder why God didn't invent a better crust for the earth. I mean, if we can invent carbon fibre, polyvinyl chloride and silicone laminates, surely he could have come up with something better than mobile rock? I mean, what gave him the idea of making Earth out of that cosmic soup and letting it cool, not in controlled conditions but in the cold vastness of space where it was bound to form a slightly dodgy crust before its centre cooled and hardened?

Nature's little jokes?

It's not just earthquakes that seem the result of bad planning.

What about hurricanes, typhoons and avalanches? We can now get out of the way of some of these, given decent warning, but wasn't it a bit mean of God to let people suffer their effects in the past before we got round to devising halfway decent weather forecasts?

And then there are volcanoes. They seem almost like sick practical jokes. You think one has been dormant for centuries. You decide it's daft not to use the fertile soil around it for farming, and then— Krakatoa!

36,000 dead.

It can't just be God keeping us on our toes, reminding us who's boss? Can it?

And what about the famines that sweep unpredictably across Africa? I don't mean those which are the result of displaced people fleeing from one region to another to escape a tyrant, but the famines that result from the complete failure of the rains that are vital to the fragile harvest?

Wind, rain and sun are all necessary, but do they have to be so erratic—causing tempest and flood one month, and drought the next? Isn't there something defective in the system?

And just as earthquakes are (as yet) outside our control, what about the diseases we've no way of curing yet? Such as life-threatening cancers or crippling arthritis, AIDS and angina? Then there are senile dementia, multiple sclerosis and, yes, backaches and the common cold. Surely they are not all the result of us abusing creation? Does God permit them just to test us, or to spur us on to more medical discoveries? Isn't that terribly hard on those who live, suffer and die before cures are perfected?

And while we're at it, why does God allow babies to be born with deformities, especially when it's to parents who have indulged in no abuse of their own bodies? And why the agonies of mental illness? Surely such suffering does not exist just to test or prove the love of those who are near and dear to the victims? Can't God organize it so that young children do not die of cancers but so that we still find ways to show courage, love and fortitude?

Why the pain of childbirth and the discomforts of old age? Why isn't it all arranged rather better?

Nature red in tooth and claw

Another thing: why do animals prey on one another? Why does the beautiful lioness track, hunt and then tear to pieces the defenceless antelope, wildebeest and zebra? Why is there a particular type of wasp that lays her eggs in the body of a caterpillar so that the wasp larvae can eat the caterpillar alive, from the inside outwards? Why, for that matter, do so many animals have to experience such terror at the sound of thunder? Is there a fault in the system?

It's not fair!

It's all so *unfair*. Of course, a bloated, self-indulgent, sixty-cigarettes-a-day, ruthless, quick-tempered businessman who treats hisstaff with contempt may 'give himself' cancer through a mixture of physical self-abuse and stress; but how does a young child 'deserve' cancer? Why do the zebra and the caterpillar have to be so unlucky?

The seeming unfairness of all this has struck people throughout history. Three thousand years ago, whoever wrote Psalm 73 was agonizing over why things go well for the wicked when he himself had not committed sin:

> *They do not suffer pain: they are strong and*
> * healthy.*
> *They do not suffer as other people do: they do*
> * not have the troubles that others have...*
> *They have plenty and are getting more.*

Devil's work

It's at this point that we have to mention the devil and ask what his role in all this might be. Nowadays, plenty of people (including many Christians) simply roar with laughter at the idea of there being a devil. The man in black, with horns and a tail, brandishing an old-fashioned toasting fork, has become a comic cartoon character, not a figure of fear.

Of course, the devil could exist without looking like that. Some people say that the devil is neither a person nor a spirit but just a source of evil. Others say that the devil exists in our own minds.

Traditionally, Satan—the devil—is said to be the chief of the fallen angels; one of a group of beings close to God who, like us, had free will. He and his friends used their freedom to refuse to obey God and were therefore cast out of heaven.

Some people say the devil wants to be equal with

God and, because of his jealousy of God, he is constantly trying to interfere in and thwart God's plans for us. It is *he*, they say, who messes up God's perfect creation with droughts, famines and earthquakes. It is he who makes one animal prey upon another—and it is he who puts evil ideas into our minds.

Indeed, the serpent who tempted Adam and Eve in the Garden of Eden is usually said to be the devil. Once they had been tempted and had eaten the forbidden fruit, so that story goes, evil and all wrongdoing came into the world. Up till then, God's creation had been perfect; there had been no sorrow or suffering.

Interestingly, the devil is mentioned more often in the New Testament than in the Old Testament: something that those Christians who don't believe in the devil might do well to remember.

◆ The devil tempted Jesus in the wilderness.

◆ He is frequently mentioned as being in opposition to Jesus in the form of demon spirits who possessed people.

◆ The apostle Peter wrote: 'Be sober, be vigilant; because your enemy, the devil, walks about like a roaring lion, seeking whom he may devour.'

◆ The apostle Paul warned us: 'Put on the whole armour of God, so that you may be able to withstand the wiles [tricks] of the devil.'

Fallen angels

So did God give his angels free will and did some therefore 'fall'? Did one of them become the devil and decide to use his freedom to hurt and damage God's creation? Is all the suffering that is not our responsibility ('natural suffering') the fault of the devil?

For some people, the answer is yes—and they can stop reading at this point. As they see it, we've just got to put up with the devil's work in this world. They believe, as the Bible suggests, that at the last judgment Satan will be sent into everlasting punishment and will do no more harm.

I'm sometimes tempted to agree with this. I certainly don't believe the devil looks like he does in the cartoons but I do believe there could be some sort of evil, fallen spirit. And just as God allows us to inflict suffering on 'lesser' creatures (the animals we hunt, trap and kill for sport or 'fun', or that we ill-treat in other ways), so might not a higher being (such as a fallen angel) hunt, tease, ill-treat and kill us?

One world

But then again, I also believe that God is good and that God created the world and all that's in it— which must include the devil. So did God create evil? Or did he just allow it to happen?

We'll come back to this idea in Chapter 9 but for the moment I have to say that I find it very hard to split creation into two halves. The whole ecosystem, or whatever you like to call it, all seems to be so wondrously interlocking that I can't imagine it being the work of two beings.

If I praise God for inspiring rainbows, beautiful sunsets and loving parents, must I not also accept the Earth's dodgy crust, volcanoes and even illness as being part of his creation? Can I still hold on to the idea that God loves us?

More questions

These problems brings us back to the big question: why does a loving God allow us to suffer things for which we're not responsible?

And that, in turn, raises six related questions:

◆ Is God in fact *not* loving, despite what Jesus said? Is he in reality rather cruel, or at least uncaring?

◆ Does suffering exist partly to keep us humble and partly to make us use our intelligence to improve the world?

◆ Does suffering exist so that we have opportunities to be caring, self-sacrificing and helpful to those in distress?

◆ Does suffering exist simply to make us appreciate how many good things there are in the world and how many good times we have?

◆ Is this actually the best possible world? Did that cosmic soup exist *before* God came along? Is what we've got the best possible thing he could make out of the raw materials he found?

and finally:

◆ Is God not 'almighty'? Could it just be that he's not actually in total control?

Enough questions. It's almost time to start looking for answers. But first we need to be sure we want answers. It could just be that things are all right as they are.

Summing up ...

Some suffering really cannot be our fault. It is this so-called 'natural' suffering that poses the really big questions.

4

Square Circles

If bees make honey, why don't ants make ketchup?

In an ideal creation, couldn't such busy, organized creatures as ants do something very much more useful than they do now? One wouldn't mind having them around the place quite so much if, every so often, you could harvest a helping of ketchup.

And while we're imagining how we could have ordered things if only we'd been planning creation, what about a world with no dangerous animals, a world with no harsh winters, no earthquakes, floods or famines—in fact, a world without suffering? What about a world that was really *safe*?

Once upon a time, there was a wealthy man who had a large number of children, but whose wife had died. As he had to go away for long periods of time, he made careful plans for their care and education. He dreaded any harm that might come to them or that they might be influenced by wicked people, so he built them a large, comfortable house in a beautiful part of the country. He hired nurses, gardeners, cooks and teachers to look after them. He then settled his children into their new home where they had everything they could possibly want.

He provided ponies for them to ride, choosing only safe, docile animals that would not throw their riders. He built walls and fences at the top of some steep cliffs in the district, and installed devices that emitted warning sounds if the children wandered into any other dangerous area. He also told his staff to watch over his children at all times, to tell them what to do and to take great care of them.

Then he went off on a long journey.

Three years passed and the father returned. It was a happy reunion. All the children were well and they had all grown taller. There had been no serious accidents or illnesses and the children had made steady progress with their schooling. All the same, the father sensed there was something wrong. The children were so quiet and listless. They seemed to have no enthusiasm for anything; nothing seemed to excite them or interest them.

He decided what he must do. He gave all the staff a month's notice and told the children they must look after themselves in the future. There would be food for a year but they'd have to cook it themselves. After that, it would be up to them. They'd have nothing to eat unless they grew it themselves. He replaced the docile ponies with horses and had some of the estate's safety devices removed. Then he went off on his own again.

At first the children were delighted. It was great fun to have no one around to tell them what to do. They could eat what they liked, when they liked and as much as they liked.

Soon, however, they found it wasn't as much fun as they'd thought.

They made terrible mistakes when they were cooking and occasionally they became ill. Nor were they brilliant at farming. In the second year they nearly starved because they did not tend the crops properly. One boy fell from a tree and broke his arm. A girl was thrown from her horse and fractured her leg. Another boy went too near the edge of the cliff and fell to his death.

When their father returned at the end of the second three years, the children had all suffered a great deal. He was grieved to hear of their tragedies and to find that they had met so much trouble. But he was pleased to see that his children were now very much more alert, very much wiser and more mature. They had grown inwardly as well as physically.

This parable describes the relationship of a loving father to his children. It is not an exact parallel to the way Christians believe God relates to us, but it does help us to focus on the question, 'Would we like to live in a world without suffering?'

Just how much would we like the world to be altered if only we had the power? Would we really want to re-order things so that nothing unpleasant ever happened in our daily lives?

No pain

Imagine, for example, a world in which there was no physical pain (remembering the distinction I made in the introduction between pain and suffering). At first it seems a lovely idea.

But without pain, we should have no early warning system when something was going wrong with our bodies. We'd have no headaches to warn us of stress or tension. No toothache to warn of an abscess. No pain in our stomachs to warn of over-indulgence or more serious internal problems. No hangovers to teach us that we'd overdone it the previous night. And without pain, how would we know when we had to rest so that a part of the body will heal itself? Yes, pain can be useful.

Furthermore, it can be a deterrent—stopping us from carrying out a physical activity that could damage the body. Through pain, we learn the danger of fire, of sharp knives, falling rocks and other hard objects. We learn how to take care of our fleshy, vulnerable bodies in a world full of very much harder objects.

Yes, pain can indeed be useful. Even necessary. So, after all, perhaps we *don't* want a world without pain. But suppose we could alter creation on a much bigger scale. How do you fancy living in one of these worlds?

◆ World 1
A world without birth or death, a world with a set number of people, a world which eventually we could make perfect and then there would be nothing further to do.

◆ **World 2**
   A world without birth or death, a world with
   a set number of people, a world which we could
   go on making better and better for ever and
   ever.

◆ **World 3**
   A world with birth but without death, a world
   which would get more and more crowded.

◆ **World 4**
   A world with birth and death, a world which
   each generation can improve or spoil, more or less
   as it chooses.

I suspect everyone will want to rule out World 3 at
once. I guess that, after a bit of thought, most people
will also want to rule out World 1. I also want to rule
out World 2. If there was no death, I fear:

◆ We would never get anything done; we'd always
   be putting it off till tomorrow.

◆ Young people would never get a chance to do
   anything: the old would make sure they remained
   in charge of everything.

◆ We could inflict unlimited suffering, world without
   end, on one another.

◆ There would no opportunities for the ultimate self-
   sacrifice of laying down one's life to save another.

◆ God wouldn't really be trusting us.

The facts of death

As a Christian, I believe that there is something after death: a new life in what we can conveniently call heaven. I know that saying 'I believe' is not a step that everyone can take. But, even if we believe death is the end of everything, I suspect that most of us are ready to accept that death is a necessary part of existence, if we really think about it. So we have to settle for World 4, including the fact of death.

I know it is easy to say that when we are not grieving for the loss of someone dear to us, or when we're young or in middle life and there seems to be plenty of time left. But I also know from experience it is not so easy when a loved one has just been snatched away and we're bitterly lonely; not so easy when someone near us fears he might be dying prematurely. Yet I still believe that death is necessary. And once we've accepted that, the problem of suffering does take on a new appearance.

Calcutta

Indeed, what many of us would call suffering need not always be regarded as something negative, pointless or just plain ghastly. Those who *are* suffering do often see it differently. Alison, a young aid worker in Calcutta, learned this by watching the people she was trying to help:

If you're a young mother trying to bring up six or seven children and you're wondering where the next kilo of rice is going to come from, and if you're watching your children die from tuberculosis or malnutrition, then sometimes the response to suffering is resignation. You give up. But I also met people with determination and drive, who were organizing themselves into neighbourhood groups to get drainage or to put better roofs on their houses or to get vaccination.

Often in Europe we have an image of Calcutta as complete misery, suffering and starvation. There is another side and there is a vitality and a determination in the people there.

Some flowers grow

I shall never forget meeting and interviewing someone else with firsthand experience of what I'd call real suffering. Margaret, a Roman Catholic Christian, was born with a form of muscular dystrophy which has meant she's always had very weak muscles and has never been able to dress or wash herself. I asked her if she ever asked herself, 'Why me?'

No, honestly I don't. I mean, some flowers grow OK and some don't. I think everything is for the good and is meant to be. It certainly hasn't destroyed my faith. Some things grow correctly and I didn't. It doesn't seem to have anything to do with the word 'faith'. It's only the body, after all, isn't it?

I asked Margaret if she thought of her condition as something she had to cope with in this life in order to make the next life easier.

I always feel I have been particularly lucky because I don't feel as if I am having to learn any lessons. It seems too easy. I'm afraid other people see my disability as a far worse thing than I ever do. I think my parents have suffered far more.

Margaret's faith and acceptance struck me as remarkable, especially when I asked her if she ever blamed God.

No. Never. There is never any question of blaming God.

Not a perfect world

Acceptance is, for many of us, much more difficult than it is for Margaret. But some people do feel it is important, as a Muslim teacher reminded me when I was making a radio programme about suffering:

It is not a perfect world and we were not destined to have complete happiness and complete satisfaction in this world. We will have that, we hope, in the world to come.

So has God deliberately made a less than perfect world? All right, he's given us pain to teach us to keep our hands out of the fire, but has he also given us disappointments to teach us to persevere—like the children in the parable—and given us cruelty so we can forgive other people?

A Jewish rabbi once put it this way:

I want to live in a world where there is joy, where there is pleasure—but I don't want a world where, if I'm walking under a ladder and something is going to fall on my head, God will cancel the natural order of things and the object will be suspended in space until I go past. It is part of the natural process of life, the mystery of life.

A safe world?

Again, as the parable of the wealthy man and his children reminds us, part of the mystery of life is the fact that the safer the world becomes, the fewer challenges it presents. The safer the world becomes, the more restricted our freedom is. The more luxurious it becomes, the lazier and dreamier we become.

The natural order

Before we can begin to find our own answers to the question of why there is suffering in the world, we must accept the way the world is; what the rabbi called the natural order.

Birds don't need eight legs so there's no point their wishing for them—just as an octopus has no need to fly. Nor is there any need for ants to make ketchup.

Thanks to our minds and our brains, there is a lot we can do to improve our lives and those of other people. We can reduce suffering and this is a point to which I shall return in Chapter 8. But we must also accept some things for what they are. Try as we like, we can't make square circles.

Nevertheless, could God have made a square circle? Could he not have arranged things in ways we can't imagine so that we had our free will and so that the natural order was maintained—but *without* things going wrong, without there being so much suffering?

We're back at the questions we asked at the end of the last chapter, and now it really is time to find out how different people have tried to answer those questions.

Summing up . . .

Out of his love for us, God has given us free will. We would be less than human without it, so we have to accept the consequences and responsibilities of having free will. We also have to accept the natural order of the universe.

5

Just as a Caterpillar . . .

Just as a caterpillar, when it comes to the end of a blade of grass, reaches out to another blade of grass and draws itself over to it; so the Soul, leaving one body and unwisdom behind, reaches out to another body and draws itself over to it.

These words come from the scriptures of the Hindu religion, the *Upanishads*. They illustrate the Hindu belief in reincarnation—the idea that the soul is reborn after death. According to the Hindu faith, if you have been very good indeed during your past life, then your soul goes straight to God. If, however, you have been sinful and done any wicked deed, then your soul is reborn in another living being on Earth. If you have committed *very* serious sins, then you are reborn very low down on the scale of life—perhaps as an animal. If, on the other hand, your actions have only been moderately sinful, then you'll be reborn as another human being but at a humbler level in life.

Hindus also believe that memories of your past life are usually wiped out at the moment of birth. Special skills or talents are thought sometimes to be carried over and, when this happens, the reborn person grows up to be a genius. If the gift that is carried over is holiness, then the reborn person may die young; The Hindu explanation is that God is ready to receive this particular soul.

When innocent people suffer, it is believed to be because they were sinful in a past life, and because those sins—which have been carried over—have to be paid for.

Because of these beliefs, death is not regarded by Hindus as it is by many people in the West. For the Hindu, death can even be something to look forward to because it is a step towards a new life. Suffering can also be welcomed, because it will earn a better life next time round and it may even be a step towards that final escape from the round of reincarnation.

So, for the followers of the great religion of India, one of the oldest religions in the world, suffering is not a problem. Everything turns out fairly in the long run and, anyway, it's all up to the individual. Even so-called natural suffering is seen either as someone's fault or as a way of earning merit. What matters is not a trouble-free life on Earth, but living life in order to achieve that eventual escape from the circle of birth and death into the infinite.

Hinduism, therefore, offers a complete and easy answer to the problem of suffering. It's so easy that it's quite tempting to accept it. Except for one thing.

You've got to give up the idea that your soul is unique to you.

Unique

For Christians, each person is separate, individual. Each of us is uniquely made in the image of God, so each person is a 'one-off'. One lifetime, from birth to death, encompasses all our experience, including the suffering we experience and inflict on others, so each human being is distinct—and immortal.

Nevertheless, it is interesting to realize that Hinduism has found an answer to our question that satisfies its followers.

So, too, has Buddhism. Indeed, the problem of suffering was its actual starting point.

Gautama

The founder of Buddhism was a Hindu prince who is said to have lived six centuries before Jesus.

The prince's name was Siddhartha Gautama. His father tried to protect him from the harsh realities of the world and from any knowledge of suffering by keeping him shut inside a very splendid palace. After some years, the prince predictably became restless, so the king decided to arrange an excursion worthy of his son's dignity.

The prince travelled by royal chariot, and as he

journeyed the people cheered him. Then he noticed one man in particular.

'That man over there,' he said to the charioteer. 'What's the matter with him?'

'He's old, my lord. That's all.'

'All?'

'Old age does that to everyone.'

'I did not realize,' said the prince thoughtfully. 'That is how age destroys beauty and youth?'

'That is so.'

The prince ordered the chariot back to the palace at once.

'How can I enjoy a journey when my heart is afraid of old age?' he said to himself.

Nevertheless, the following day, he insisted on making another journey. Once again his attention was attracted by a person at the roadside. Again he asked his charioteer to explain.

'That, my lord, is a leper,' came the answer.

'Is that what men call disease?'

'That is what disease can do to a man.'

On the third day's journey, the prince hoped to see no more suffering but on this occasion he saw four men carrying something.

'That,' my lord, explained the charioteer, 'is a corpse. That is the end which has been fixed for us all.'

The prince was so distressed that he left the palace permanently, gave up his wealth and lived as a wandering hermit, trying to find an answer to our question: 'Why should there be suffering in the world?'

One day in his search for the meaning of life he came upon a great tree.

'I shall sit beneath this tree,' he said, 'and though my flesh and bones should waste away and my life-blood dry, I shall not stir again until I have found the truth.'

At daybreak, the truth was revealed to him and he became the Buddha, which means 'the enlightened one'.

For the Buddha, there were four 'Noble Truths' discovered through his enlightenment:

◆ In this world, nothing lasts. Even the happiest moments pass away. Nobody experiences total and permanent happiness or satisfaction. The Buddhist word for this unsatisfactoriness of life is *dukkha*, a word which means both 'restlessness' and 'suffering'.

◆ *Dukkha* happens because people want to keep things. They want more and more and are never satisfied. They become greedy and selfish. If countries become greedy and selfish, this leads to war.

◆ *Dukkha* can cease if you overcome your selfishness, greed and hatred.

◆ The way to achieve this is to follow the 'Eightfold Path'.

And the Eightfold Path was the Buddha's second set of teachings. Each can be summed up in two words:

◆ *Right view*: Understand yourself; see what you're doing with life.

◆ *Right thought*: Think how you can be of use.

◆ *Right speech*: Speak the truth; say good things to and about other people.

◆ *Right actions*: Be straightforward and generous in your actions.

◆ *Right livelihood*: Choose a job which does not harm other living beings.

◆ *Right effort*: Use your mind and strength to cut through difficulties.

◆ *Right mindfulness*: Take care of everybody you meet.

◆ *Right concentration*: Look beneath the surface of life to try to find the source of your own existence.

A Buddhist monk speaks

In the light of this teaching, what is the Buddhist answer to the question of suffering? For Tew Bunnag, a Buddhist monk, there is no problem:

The fact is that we grow old, we die, we decay. This is something which we must accept first of all.

The Buddhist looks at life with this complete sense of reality. For him to say that we grow old and we decay and we die is not a melancholy thing, it's not a sad thing. It's like saying, 'In autumn the leaves fall'.

When I've spoken to Buddhists about this, they have often seemed to me to be remarkably cheerful in the face of disaster. To quote Tew Bunnag again:

The Buddhist way makes you cheerful. If you can truly accept the disaster of your life, that you are growing old and you cannot cling to anything, you become light, you feel light. Suffering is not something that you turn away from. It's not something that you drug yourself against.

Resignation to suffering and the acceptance of death as a natural occurrence may seem alien to Western people, but there is much the Christian can learn from the Buddhist. (We shall return to this point in Chapter 8.)

Acceptance, as a response to suffering, is found in several other of the world's great religions. Indeed, it is the keynote of the Muslim religion. The very name, *Islam*, means 'resignation' or 'submission to the divine will'.

The world of Islam

Islam's greatest prophet was Muhammad, who lived from 570 to 632AD, and it teaches that God has control over all creation. The Muslim's proper reaction to suffering must be acceptance and submission. This teaching can be illustrated by a story about a Muslim who was told that one of his seven children had died. His first reaction was to say, 'Thank God that he has left six for me.' Muslims should count their blessings rather than fret about what they have lost. As it says in the Muslim holy book, the Qur'an:

When a blow strikes you… will you say,
'Why has this happened?'
Say: 'It is from your own selves. Truly God
has power over every single thing.'

Since God is in control of everything, he is responsible for suffering. To quote the Qur'an again:

There is no kind of blow [or affliction] *except*
by the leave of God…

Because Islam teaches that God is all-powerful, his purpose cannot be thwarted. You cannot hope to avoid his will, as this parable reveals.

One day a man was visiting the court of the great King Solomon. While he was there, he saw the Angel of Death also present. Believing that the Angel of Death was looking at him angrily, he privately asked King Solomon to send him at once by magic to far-distant India. The King granted him his request.

The King (who also knew that the Angel of Death was present) then turned to the Angel.

'Were you indeed looking on that man with anger?'

'Oh no,' replied the Angel of Death. 'I was looking at him not in anger but in surprise. You see, I am under orders to kill him today—in India.'

According to Islam, there is no escaping the will of God or the will of Allah (to use the Arabic word for God).

Trial and punishment

The Qur'an also shows how suffering fulfils two of God's purposes: the first is to serve as a punishment for our wrongdoing.

When El Asnam in Algeria was devastated by an earthquake, an *Imam* (a minister or priest) had no hesitation in explaining it:

It's an act of God because everything that happens on earth and in the sky comes from God. It's a punishment in the sense that a lot of people have left the way of God and have brought the need for punishment upon us— but it's also a warning for people to return to the way of God.

The second purpose of suffering, according to Islam (and this helps to explain the reason for un-deserved or natural suffering), is that it is a test or trial of the faithful. The Qur'an describes days when suffering afflicts us in this way:

Such days are dealt out among men in turn that God may know those who believe, and that he may take from among you witnesses... that God may prove those who believe and bruise those who disbelieve.

If those who do wrong often appear to escape suffering, the Qur'an assures Muslim believers that there will be a reckoning after death and that the sufferings of hell can be far worse than those on Earth. As a commentator and writer on Islam, Riadh El Droubie, points out:

Muslims do pray to God to punish them in this life instead of punishing them in the hereafter and we accept that punishment here means being saved from punishment in the hereafter.

For Muslims, (Riadh El Droubie suggests) this again helps to explain undeserved and natural suffering:

Take for example an earthquake. A lot of innocent people are killed. They don't suffer without a reward to compensate their suffering.

*In war a lot of people, innocent people,
sometimes get killed. If they are fighters in
God's cause, we call them martyrs and God
will reward them. But victims who have no
part in the fighting are also sometimes killed.
God again will reward them to compensate for
suffering on this earth. Their reward will come
in the next life.*

It must be pointed out that Islam does not teach its
followers to ignore suffering completely. One of
the five pillars or commands of the faith is to give
to the poor and needy. Muslims are commanded to
do what they can to relieve poverty, distress and in-
justice. As a Muslim lecturer, Dr Abdel Halleem, says,

*If you can control suffering, you must do
everything you can. If it is physical suffering,
you must go to the doctor; you are ordered to do
that by Islam. God does expect us to use modern
science to improve the world. Certainly.*

Blessed are the poor

As I say, the acceptance of suffering that is ex-
pected by religions such as Hinduism, Buddhism
and Islam may not come easily to people in the
West. There is, however, a logic about the Islamic
view that does remove the problem for the faithful
Muslim. And there are similarities between its
teaching and certain Christian texts. The belief

that we shall be rewarded in the next world for un-
due suffering in this world is very close to Jesus'
teaching: 'Blessed are the poor in spirit, for theirs
is the kingdom of heaven.' Jesus also said:

> *Blessed are those who are persecuted for
> righteousness' sake, for theirs is the kingdom
> of heaven. Blessed are you when men revile
> you and persecute you and utter all kinds of
> evil against you falsely on my account. Rejoice
> and be glad, for your reward is great in heaven.*

What Christianity does *not* teach is that suffering is a
punishment from God. People once asked Jesus if a
man who had been born blind was afflicted because
he was sinful or because his parents had been sinful.
Jesus replied firmly that it was for neither reason.
Rather it was so that God's power might be seen at
work in him.

Even so, the idea of suffering as a form of
punishment or warning *is* present in the Bible—at
least in the Old Testament.

Summing up . . .

For the Hindu, suffering is a way of reaching God.

For the Buddhist, suffering must be accepted as
natural.

For the Muslim, suffering can be a punishment, a
test or a way of earning merit.

The Christian may or may not accept these ideas . . .

6

Job and his Comforters

If we read the Old Testament, the Bible of the Jewish people, we can't get away from it: God punishes people. When his chosen people (as the Jews are described) do wrong, disaster strikes. Indeed, God is repeatedly described as being 'vengeful' (which the dictionary defines as 'disposed to revenge'). And not just once or twice—there are plenty of such references:

Thou God of vengeance...
An avenger of their wrongdoing...
I will punish the world for its evil and the
  wicked for their sinfulness...

... and so on.

Jeremiah

In the Old Testament, the prophets or teachers of the Jewish people warn everyone about this vengeance. 'If you do not follow God's will,' say the prophets, 'you will be punished.'

For example, in the Book of Jeremiah, we can read how the prophet Jeremiah predicted that God would punish his people if they persisted in their wrongdoing. Jeremiah told them:

> *You do one evil thing after another. You steal, you murder, you commit adultery, tell lies under oath, offer sacrifices to false gods and do not acknowledge your God. You must change your way of life.*

But they didn't. Jeremiah then predicted what God would do.

> *The Lord God says, 'I will make Jerusalem a pile of ruins. I will send armies against you and I will scatter you among the nations.'*

The people failed to change their ways even then and so, according to Jeremiah, they were punished. The second Book of Chronicles tells of the disasters which then beset the Jewish people. In the year 597 BC, King Nebuchadnezzar of Babylonia turned up, complete with his army, and attacked the capital city of Jerusalem. He set up camp outside the city and built siege walls around it so that no one could get in or out. After several months, the famine in the city had become so bad that the people had nothing left to eat. Nebuchadnezzar then attacked the city, breaking down its walls.

He had the young men killed and showed little mercy on anyone, young or old. He looted the temple, the temple treasury and the palace, seizing everything that was made of gold or silver. He then burnt down the temple and palace, and destroyed the remains of the city walls. He took the survivors back to Babylonia where they had to serve him and his descendants as slaves.

Quite a punishment.

A punishment from God?

The idea that God punishes us when we do wrong is not confined to the Jewish faith. As we have seen, this belief is also found in Islam. Some Christians also believe that God intervenes in this way. Preachers have argued, even in modern times, that certain disasters are God's punishment for our wrongdoing. Most notably, some people have said that AIDS is God's punishment for sexual immorality.

If we accept that suffering is a punishment, then there's no problem, no mystery. It means that we bring all suffering on ourselves. It's as if all suffering is of the first type, the type we discussed in Chapter 1. Nebuchadnezzar's attack on Jerusalem and AIDS are both like the Holocaust or Cambodia. Suffering has come as the result of our wickedness. There's no problem. Except that AIDS, for example, is a pretty unfair punishment (if it is one). Why should God punish male but not female homosexuals, and why should he punish drug addicts who inject but not those who don't?

Can we really accept the idea that suffering is a punishment sent by God?

If we're Jewish, can we really believe that God would do such things to his own, chosen people? If we're Christian, we're back with our big question: why does a loving God allow such things to happen—especially when it affects those who don't seem to deserve it?

No obvious reason

Take the experience of Canon Trevor Beeson, whom I once interviewed about this question of punishment. It concerned him very directly, as he told me:

> *My daughter's husband was killed just nine months after they were married. They'd had a lovely wedding in Westminster Abbey, a fairy-tale situation, and they were very much in love. Nine months later he was killed in a car accident for no obvious reason. The explanation of it will never be forthcoming. He wasn't drunk. He wasn't driving fast. He didn't bang into anything else but for some quite inexplicable reason the car ran off the road and crashed into a wall and he was killed instantly.*

Why should such a tragedy hit this particular family?

The story of Job

The Old Testament, for all its references to a 'vengeful' God, does address itself to this very human question—especially in the Book of Job. Job was an honourable person who worshipped God and did no wrong. He helped the poor and the sick and gave help to anyone in need. He was humble and faithful to God.

Then he suffered a series of catastrophes. His oxen and camels were killed. His sheep were struck by lightning. His sons and daughters were killed when the house they were in was struck by a whirlwind. Amazingly, Job still trusted in God. 'I was born with nothing and I will die with nothing. The Lord gave and now he takes away. Blessed be the name of the Lord.'

Job then became ill himself. His body was covered with sores. Still he said nothing against God. 'When God sends us something good, we welcome it. How can we complain when he sends us trouble?'

However, Job suffered so much and for so long that eventually he did curse the day he was born—and he asked the question we've been asking.

'I wish I'd died in my mother's womb or died the moment I was born. Why did I live to suffer?'

Three of his friends, Eliphaz, Bildad and Zophar, offered possible answers.

◆ Firstly, Eliphaz gave him the traditional Old Testament answer. He told Job that he *must* have done wrong because only the wicked suffer—and so he must accept his punishment. 'I have seen people plough fields of evil and sow wickedness like

seed. Like a storm, God destroys them in his anger.'
Eliphaz went on to suggest something not unlike
what was to become Muslim teaching on the
subject some centuries later. 'Happy is the person
whom the Lord God corrects! Don't resent it when
he rebukes you.'

◆ Secondly, Bildad suggested that God would put
everything right in the end and Job must simply be
patient. 'God never twists justice. Your children
must have sinned against God and so he punished
them as they deserved. Turn and plead with God. If
you are honest and pure, God will help you and all
your past wealth will be nothing to what God will
give you. God never abandons the faithful. He will
let you laugh and shout again.'

◆ Thirdly, Zophar argued that really Job deserved to
suffer far more. 'You claim you are pure in the sight
of God! No, God is punishing you far less than you
deserve! God knows which men are worthless. He
sees all their evil deeds.'

Which may all have been very true, but it wasn't
much comfort (hence the term 'Job's comforters',
meaning people who aren't much comfort).

Satan suggests . . .

One thing the Book of Job never suggests (as some
religions do) is that everything will be put right in

the next life. Another point it's equally clear about is that it is God who allows suffering.

Indeed, the Book of Job begins with a conversation between God and Satan (or the devil), in which Satan suggests that Job is righteous only because he finds he prospers by being so. Satan asks God's permission to test Job by causing all the suffering he has to undergo. Is the Book of Job going further than saying suffering is a punishment, by suggesting that it is a test of faith (as Bildad implies)?

What's more, does that argument make any sense today? Can we accept that God lets us suffer just to test our faith?

The Holocaust

Take such a terrible tragedy as the Holocaust, in which so many Jews perished.

It was, of course, caused by evil people. It was not started by God. Even so, he 'let it happen'. Did he allow it, either as a punishment or a test of faith? I once put that question to the late Moshe Davis, then Executive Director of the Chief Rabbi's Office:

If we are wicked and we do not do the will of God, then we shall suffer. That is our teaching. But it's very hard, of course, to relate this to something like the Holocaust. Hard, I would say, almost to the degree of being impossible because we cannot accept that so many people, innocent people, with probably about a million children amongst them, suffered in this way as part of the fulfilment of God's will.

But what I do accept is the concept that if we as a nation do that which is right, then we are entitled, as it were, to prosperity. But if we are divided amongst ourselves and we are not dealing with our neighbours as we ought to do, then the nation as a whole will suffer and eventually go under.

Prosperity for believers?

It is worth pointing out that, despite Jesus' teaching that God forgives rather than punishes us for sins (provided we own up to them and are sorry), there *are* some Christians who agree with Moshe Davis that God does reward the faithful by making them prosperous and wealthy in this world.

Job knew otherwise

But let's go back to the story of Job and his would-be comforters. All three of them were sure (for different reasons) that Job must have brought his suffering on himself. In some ways, their answers are perfectly logical. They make sense.

In his heart, however, Job knew otherwise. Although he had been sinful, he had tried to live an honest and upright life. He knew he had committed no great crime, nothing to merit such punishment.

And like so many people, he was lonely in his suffering. He tried to feel in touch with God—without success. In his despair, he could not find God. Even so, his faith held firm in that he believed, deep down, that God had not abandoned him totally.

Eventually, in his frustration, Job challenged God to answer him—and, in the story, God confronted him. Not surprisingly, Job was nervous.

But all God did was to remind Job of the greatness of God and the complex, magnificent mystery of creation.

Job then had to answer God:

I know, Lord, that you are all-powerful, that you can do anything you want. You ask how I dare question your wisdom when I am so very ignorant.

I talked about things I did not understand, about marvels too great for me to know.

You told me to listen while you spoke and to try to answer your questions. Then I knew only what others had told me, but now I have seen you with my own eyes. I am ashamed of all I have said—and I repent.

Beyond our understanding

Job realized that God is not only all-powerful but beyond human understanding. Job accepted that God has a plan—but not one the human mind can grasp. We cannot predict divine action. We cannot make sense of God. He is too big, too complex, for us to understand.

So Job fell silent, surrendering to divine love. A clever, worked-out answer was not on. Job just had to accept things as he found them, without questioning.

Don't ask!

So is the moral that we, like Job, are wrong even to be asking these questions? Should we not simply say, 'The mystery of why there is suffering is too difficult for our poor little brains to understand. We can't work out the answer. We must just accept—and trust!'? Like the Buddhist, like the Muslim, like Job: must we accept?

Ah, but the Book of Job is not the Bible's only word on the subject, marvellous though the story is. It's not even the Old Testament's only word. There is also the little matter of the scapegoat...

Summing up...

One response to the problem of suffering is to say that it is a mystery we must accept and not question.

7

Scapegoats

I suspect (and also pray) that very few people reading this book will ever have to experience the
worst kinds of suffering. The suffering that we
see all too often in the television news bulle-
tins—suffering like that of a whole tribe or nation
dying of famine in the midst of an African drought.
Or suffering like that of the people of Sarajevo in
Bosnia who suddenly found their familiar streets
had become a battle-ground in a bloody civil war.

Yet even if we are spared such major disasters,
most of us still have our private griefs—agonies of
pain for which there seems no relief. There is the
hurt that comes when a much loved member of the
family rejects us or takes against us. There is the
loneliness that comes with the death of a loved
one—whether it's the sudden shock of an unex-
pected accident or fatal heart attack, or 'simply' the
end of a long and happy life.

And often it is the *loneliness* that's so hard to
bear. The fact is that the rest of the world is going

about its business. But there we are. Alone. In our sorrow.

And then there's the anxiety of possible future suffering. Growing old. Losing our physical faculties and strength... Perhaps dying alone.

It's scary.

Except that, for the Christian, there is an assurance that we are not alone.

Aaron and the goat

Besides the Book of Job, there is another Old Testament answer to the question of how we can be relieved of our suffering. This goes right back to the time of Moses, before the Israelites came to live in Palestine. It is described in a book of the Bible called Leviticus and it is known as the ceremony of the scapegoat. It was first performed by Aaron, the brother of Moses.

When Aaron has finished performing the ritual to purify the Most Holy Place, he shall offer to the Lord the live goat, and shall put both his hands on the goat's head and confess over it all the evils, sins and rebellions of the people of Israel, and so transfer them to the goat's head. Then the goat is to be driven off into the desert by a man appointed to do so. The goat will carry all their sins away with it into some uninhabited land.

It seems a bit hard on the goat! More seriously, though, here in this early ritual is a reminder that God wanted to give his people a way of dealing with the terrors of suffering and the problem of evil. He wanted to provide a means by which we could be made free.

▨ The servant of the Lord

Over the years, the scapegoat ceremony changed. Much later in the Old Testament, a prophet called Isaiah described a mysterious figure who was yet to come. He would be the servant of the Lord. He would be the new scapegoat.

In this passage, although Isaiah was describing what were future events to him, he spoke as if the new scapegoat had already come.

He endured the suffering that should have been ours, the pain that we should have borne. All the while we thought that his suffering was punishment sent by God. But because of our sins he was wounded, beaten because of the evil we did. We are healed by the punishment he suffered, made whole by the blows he received. All of us were like sheep that were lost, each of us going his own way. But the Lord made the punishment fall on him, the punishment all of us deserved.

He was treated harshly, but endured it humbly; he never said a word. Like a lamb about to be slaughtered, like a sheep about to be sheared, he never said a word. He was arrested and sentenced and led off to die, and no one cared about his fate. He was put to death for the sins of our people. He was placed in a grave with evil men, he was buried with the rich, even though he had never committed a crime or ever told a lie.

Isaiah 53:4–9

In many ways, the suffering servant is just like the scapegoat, carrying away the suffering of the people. In many more ways the suffering servant is like Jesus—and Christians do, in fact, take this description to be a prophecy about him.

The life of Jesus

Christians believe that, in Jesus, God was born on Earth, as a Jew. His life was not easy. There was gossip about him even before he was born: his mother's husband was an old man and, well, you know what people say . . .

When he was thirty, he started travelling through the countryside and the towns. He taught, preached and healed the sick. He did no harm. He did no wrong. He did only good.

Even so, after three years, various people grew jealous of him. He became the victim of their prejudice and hatred. They soon found a chance to arrest him, torture him and put him on trial.

They accused him falsely, whipped him, beat him up—and sentenced him to death.

He was treated harshly, but endured it humbly; he never said a word. Like a lamb about to be slaughtered, like a sheep about to be sheared, he never said a word.

And he was led off to die. By crucifixion.

The death of Jesus

He was made to carry the crossbeam of his own cross through the city. He was laughed at and spat upon.

Then he was stretched out on the ground and his wrists were nailed to the crossbeam. He and the beam were then hoisted up and secured to the upright post. He was nailed through his feet and stabbed in the side. And there he was left to die while the crowds jeered at him. Even though he had never committed a crime or told a lie.

The long silence

Now imagine the end of time. All the people who have ever lived and suffered on this earth are impatient to accuse the supposedly loving God of the many things that they have had to undergo. The charge they bring against God is that he doesn't know what they've been through...

84

At the end of time, billions of people were scattered on a great plain before God's throne. Most shrank back from the brilliant light before them. But some groups near the front talked heatedly—not with cringing shame, but with belligerence.

'How can God judge us? How can he know about suffering?' snapped a young brunette. She ripped open a sleeve to reveal a tattooed number from a Nazi concentration camp. 'We endured terror . . . beatings . . . torture . . . death!'

In another group a black boy lowered his collar. 'What about this?' he demanded, showing an ugly rope burn. 'Lynched for no crime but being black! We have suffocated in slave ships, been wrenched from loved ones, toiled till only death gave release.'

In another group, a young girl stared with sullen eyes. On her forehead was the stamp 'illegitimate'. 'To endure my stigma,' she murmured, 'was beyond, beyond . . .' and her voice trailed off, to be taken up by others.

Far out across the plain were hundreds of such groups. Each had a complaint against God for the evil and suffering he permitted in his world. How lucky God was to live in heaven where all was sweetness and light, where there was no weeping, no fear, no hunger, no hatred. Indeed, what did God know of what humanity had been forced to endure in this world? After all, God leads a pretty sheltered life, they said.

So each of these groups sent forth a leader, chosen because of having suffered the most. There was a Jew, a black woman, an 'untouchable', an illegitimate child, a man horribly deformed by arthritis, a citizen of Hiroshima, and a victim of a Serbian slave camp. In the centre of the plain they consulted with each other. At last they were ready to present their case. It was quite simple. Before God would be qualified to be their judge, he must endure what they had endured. Their decision was that God *should be sentenced to live on earth—as a human being*!

But, because he was God, they set certain safeguards to be sure he could not use his divine powers to help himself.

'Let him be born a Jew.'

'Let the legitimacy of his birth be doubted so that none will know who is really his father.'

'Give him a work so difficult that even his family will think he is out of his mind when he tries to do it.'

'Let him try to describe what no other man has ever seen, tasted, heard or smelled. Let him try to describe God to people.'

'Let him be betrayed by his dearest friends.'

'Let him be indicted with false charges, tried before a prejudiced jury, convicted by a cowardly judge.'

'At last, let him see what it means to be terribly alone, completely abandoned by every living thing.'

'Let him be tortured, and then let him die.'

'Let him die so that there can be no doubt that he died.'

'Let there be a great crowd to verify it.'

As each leader announced his portion of the sentence, loud murmurs of approval went up from the great throng of people assembled. But when the last had finished pronouncing sentence, there was a long silence.

No one uttered a word.

No one moved.

For suddenly all knew.

God had already served his sentence.

'I know how you feel'

Part of the Christian answer to the problem of suffering is this: whatever happens to us, we know that God himself has been through it all in the person of Jesus.

I remember when a friend of mine, Ralph, lost his father to whom he was very close. He told me that several people, in offering their condolences, said the same thing, 'I know just how you must be feeling.' And Ralph made the point that those words meant far more when they came from someone who had lost a parent themselves than when they came from someone whose parents were both living.

God *does* know what it is to suffer. He knows how we feel.

Not such a punishment?

Yes, I know there will be those who say that, in comparison with someone who is systematically tortured for years in an illegal jail, the sufferings of Jesus were quite short-lived. He was arrested one

Thursday evening and executed on Friday, dying much more rapidly than most crucifixion victims—after just three hours on the cross.

But behind his physical suffering there was a greater agony—the agony of:

◆ knowing that he had been betrayed by one friend and deserted by others;

◆ knowing that his loving mother was watching his agony;

◆ knowing her suffering;

◆ knowing what it is to be human and to doubt, to wonder if God had forsaken him;

◆ knowing that, despite the sightseeing crowds, he was alone, rejected by those he had come to help and save;

◆ knowing that all the work he had done—the teaching, the healing, the helping—was, for the moment, as nothing;

◆ knowing that he was innocent; knowing it was all so unfair;

◆ knowing that he was the scapegoat for everyone else . . .

God *does* know what it is to suffer.

God suffers now.

And God knows what it is to suffer not only through his life on Earth as Jesus. God has suffered with us in the past, he is suffering with us now, and he will go on suffering to the end of time. As Jesus said, 'Look at these two sparrows. They're worth very little. But not one of them will fall to the ground without your Father being there. You are worth a lot more to God than the birds of the air.'

Like a loving parent who suffers when his or her child is in pain, so God suffers for us. Even when he seems to be silent, he hears our prayers. That is the message of Christianity.

And like a loving parent who knows that children grow up, and that there is a time to let them go their own ways, so God has given us free will to go our own ways. Like a loving parent who longs to interfere in his or her grown-up children's lives when they make mistakes, so too God watches us. And how he suffers when we do.

Summing up . . .

Whatever else Christianity teaches, it is that we are not alone. Through Jesus Christ, God is with us in our suffering.

8

No Gain Without Pain?

Corrie and Betsie ten Boom were sisters who lived in Haarlem in Holland. When Germany invaded their country during World War II, they provided a 'safe house' for their Jewish friends and neighbours, who were being hunted by the Nazis for deportation to concentration camps. Eventually, Corrie and Betsie were themselves arrested.

They were taken to Germany, to a women's extermination camp called Ravensbrück. There, they suffered from terrible cold, from beatings, and from hunger. But they had managed to smuggle in with them something which gave them comfort and hope—a Bible.

In Ravensbrück, Corrie remembered how she had previously read the story of Jesus' arrest, of how soldiers had slapped him, laughed at him, and flogged him. 'Now I could see such happenings,' she said.

Some weeks later, the two sisters were moved to a new prison block and crowded in with a hundred other women. Among the many other hardships, they found the building was swarming with fleas. Corrie asked Betsie how they could live in such a place. Betsie's answer was to remember what it said in the Bible. 'Rejoice always, pray constantly, give thanks in all circumstances.' Betsie was determined to thank God for every single thing about the new barracks—even the fleas.

And the fleas did turn out to be a blessing. Because of them, the guards were reluctant to inspect that particular prison block and so, with the help of their smuggled Bible, Corrie and Betsie were able to hold secret services. After the war, Corrie recalled what they were like.

They were services like no others, those times in Barracks 28. We'd sing a hymn and then either Betsie or I would open the Bible and read aloud to all those people, who had been so cruelly separated from their own families. And I knew that, even in darkness, God's truth shines most clear. No matter how much we have to suffer, Jesus has suffered too. And no matter how much things go wrong, he is with us, and he will help us, and help us to help others.

In Ravensbrück, Corrie and Betsie were sustained by the Christian belief, and *experience*, that God is present with us in our suffering. As I said in the previous chapter, we are not alone. We need never feel we are alone.

What is more, by sharing in the sufferings of Jews in Haarlem and of other prisoners in Ravensbrück,

Corrie and Betsie were able to help others. Something positive resulted from their own suffering.

Which brings us to the question about whether suffering exists especially so that we may help others.

The point of pain

Let's try to answer that first by considering physical pain. When pain is courageously borne, it can ennoble a person; it can strengthen character. If you don't give in to self-pity, to moaning and whinging, you are a better person—and, just as importantly, you can inspire those around you.

'How heroic she is,' we say. 'All that pain and she never complains.' Because of her pain, our sympathy and love develop. Out of her pain comes goodness.

But an awful lot of physical pain is pretty grim. It might be the misery of lolling around in an untidy bedroom, surrounded by used handkerchiefs, as you cope with a throbbing head and a bout of flu. It might be constant and chronic back pain that leaves you whimpering into your pillow with despair... It's difficult to be noble in such circumstances—and you can also be a real trial to those who are attempting to look after you. Out of that pain can also come short tempers, tiredness and impatience.

To suggest that pain exists just so we can try to put up with it and just so that a member of the family or a nurse might feel good by helping us is, I think, plain nonsense.

Of course, it *can* provide an opportunity for the victim to be uncomplaining, it *does* provide an opportunity for others to show tender loving care—but that can't be the *point* of pain.

Grief develops the mind

But (remembering the distinction I made in the Introduction) what about *suffering*?

A French writer, Marcel Proust, made this point:

Happiness is beneficial for the body but it is grief that develops the powers of the mind.

To put it another way, we don't gain anything when our bodies are 'unhappy'—but when we experience grief or misery, or what I've been calling suffering in this book, then there is a gain.

This was also very much the view of another writer, C.S. Lewis. He compared the human being to a statue that is being shaped by a sculptor. The statue must suffer blows from the sculptor's hammer and chisel as it is shaped into perfection. Similarly, Lewis suggests that pain and suffering are blows we must suffer as we are slowly moulded into perfection.

Dr Abdel Halleem puts it from a Muslim viewpoint:

Any person can become too proud of himself. If he has a bit of suffering he will see that he is not really the semi-god he had thought himself as being.

Learning from suffering

There is no doubt that it is possible to develop, to grow, through suffering. At its simplest, the doctor who has been seriously ill is often a very much better doctor for having undergone the experience of being a patient.

Through suffering, we can all learn:

◆ patience and humility;

◆ perseverance;

◆ courage;

◆ wisdom and understanding.

Out of suffering can come the capacity both to love deeply and selflessly, and to get to know ourselves properly and honestly. The Buddhist monk, Tew Bunnag, whom I quoted in an earlier chapter, puts it this way:

By confronting suffering we confront our basic humanity, we become truly alive. Someone who cannot confront or face up to their suffering cannot be truly alive because he or she is trying to blot out an aspect of themselves which is staring them in the face every single day and every single moment. What we gain by admitting we must suffer is an insight into the reality of the world.

For Tew Bunnag, the benefit of suffering is very firmly in this world.

> *It's not as if you are going to chalk up marks in heaven, so that when you die someone says, 'Oh, yes, you have a place here because you suffered so much.' That's not the way you gain from suffering.*

▓ I want to be unhappy

Some people would go so far as to say that some suffering is necessary if we are to be fully developed. Without it, we are less than human.

In Aldous Huxley's novel *Brave New World*, the author pictures a future where there is perfect health and where science and technology have provided for every need. The result is total comfort—but most people are little more than zombies.

A character called the Savage visits this civilization and is shown all its supposed advantages. After his tour of inspection, he talks with its leaders.

'What you need,' he says, 'is something with tears for a change... Isn't there something in living dangerously?'

The reply he is given is, 'We prefer to do things comfortably.'

'But I don't want comfort,' answers the Savage. 'I want God, I want poetry, I want real danger, I want freedom, I want goodness. I want sin... I'm claiming the right to be unhappy.'

But that means other things as well—as the rulers in *Brave New World* point out:

'Not to mention the right to grow old and ugly and impotent; the right to have syphilis and cancer; the right to have too little to eat; the right to be lousy; the right to live in constant apprehension of what may happen tomorrow; the right to catch typhoid; the right to be tortured by unspeakable pains of every kind.'

After a long silence in which the Savage weighs it all up, he answers, 'I claim them all.'

Courage is infectious

Without suffering, we can so easily become less than human. Without setbacks, without problems to overcome, we do not grow. It does seem better to have some suffering than none at all.

Strange as it may seem, even our religious faith can be strengthened by suffering (as was the faith of Corrie and Betsie ten Boom; as was my own by watching my mother face her death).

Indeed, the courageous bearing of suffering can lift the morale of those around them. Courage, it seems, can be infectious.

No room for masochism

Does this mean that we must actually seek out suffering? And has God deliberately made suffering a part of creation as a way of improving us?

Frankly, I find that extraordinarily difficult to accept. I can't believe that there are wars just so that there can be heroes and heroines like the ten Boom sisters.

I can't believe there are terminal illnesses just so that some patients can die nobly and so that doctors and nurses can be caring.

I can't believe there are earthquakes and famines so that victims can be brave and stoical—and so that we can support various charities.

And I'm sorry to disagree with such a famous writer as C.S. Lewis, but I can't believe that the loving God of Christianity deliberately invented suffering just so that I might be shaped into a better person.

Growing

What I do believe is that suffering does have its uses. Since it is in the world, God has arranged things so that it can have useful by-products.

If we face up to it, as Tew Bunnag suggests and as Corrie and Betsie ten Boom did, we can grow.

That's the third time I've used the word 'grow' in this chapter. Each time, I might have used the word 'travel'.

Soul-making

Many Christian teachers and preachers have described the process of living and growing as a journey. Augustine of Hippo described life as being a journey of soul-making. Slowly, as we struggle through life we are making or developing our soul. The journey can be a struggle; it can be tiring. But life cannot stand still. There is always something more to be done, something more to be suffered—and it can become much harder going as we get older.

On the journey, our love for God and our love for one another is tested. But if we continue to trust God and care for our loved ones, our souls will mature.

When Paul wrote to the Christians at Rome, he said we were to rejoice in our sufferings because we know that suffering produces endurance, endurance produces character and character produces hope. And hope is one of the three great Christian virtues, along with faith and love.

Summing up...

Suffering does not exist in order to make us better people—but it is part of the mystery of creation that it is useful in this way.

9

Why God No Kill the Devil?

In the story *Robinson Crusoe*, by Daniel Defoe, Crusoe is shipwrecked on a desert island.

He spends many years alone there until he rescues a native of that region from being eaten by cannibals. He calls him Man Friday and begins to teach him English.

After a while he tells Friday about God and how the devil tempts people to do wrong.

'Well,' says Friday, 'but you say God is so strong, so great; is he not much strong, much might as the devil?'

'Yes, yes,' says I, 'Friday, God is stronger than the devil, God is above the devil.'

'But,' says he again, 'if God much strong, much might as the devil, why God no kill the devil, so make him do no more wicked?'

It's a good question.

Why not?

If God is 'almighty', why doesn't he put an end to the devil's evil ways? Or, if you don't believe in some kind of evil being called the devil, why doesn't God simply put an end to evil?

I began to answer this question in Chapter 4. As I said, part of the answer is that, out of his love for us, God has given us free will. If you believe in the devil, God gave even him free will! We have the freedom to behave well or badly—and God is not going to take away from us our responsibility of deciding how we behave. Nor is he going to do everything for us by intervening in the world to stop drunken drivers, careless mechanics or even power-mad dictators. Like a loving father who knows that his children must learn to be responsible for their actions, he's decided that we must take some of the blame.

All this time, we've been accepting the idea that God is all-powerful. He could do anything if he wished—even if he doesn't.

Is God in control?

I wonder if God really *is* all-powerful. Is he really in control?

The traditional Christian belief is that God *is* all-powerful and that he does actually interfere in the world from time to time. If we believe the Bible, he has indeed disrupted the normal order of things at certain times.

In the Old Testament, he sent along a few plagues to help the Israelites escape from Egypt. He parted the Red Sea so they could walk safely across it. He got his prophet Elijah to make a sopping wet bonfire, and then lit it for him.

In the New Testament, when God came to Earth as Jesus, he calmed a storm, produced a couple of miraculous picnics for huge crowds in the wilderness and even brought his friend Lazarus back from the dead.

Hands off?

But God's power seems strangely limited. If Lazarus was brought back from the dead, why weren't other followers and friends of Jesus helped in similar ways?

Why was Stephen stoned to death? Why was Peter crucified—upside down? Why were hundreds of Christians later put to death by Roman emperors? And why are devout Christians still tortured today?

To put it very kindly, either God seems to have an amazingly hands-off policy nowadays—or we have to accept that he is not all-powerful.

Three possibilities

If we decide that God is not all-powerful, there are three possibilities to consider:

◆ There are two gods, one good and one bad. We can call them God and the devil. They are equally powerful and in conflict with one another.

◆ When God undertook the creation of the universe, he made it out of chaotic matter that already existed. The world we've got is the best he could manage to make out of the material he started with.

◆ God has deliberately created the universe in such a way that he does not have complete control over it. In some mysterious way, he limited his own power.

Of these, the third is in line with what many Christians believe, and it is certainly the one I accept.

There is some truth in the other two options, however. You have only to read the New Testament to see several references to 'the powers of darkness' —strong, evil powers that God, in Jesus, must fight. As to the second option: well, the Book of Genesis does talk about God making the world out of chaos. Even so, it is the third option that seems most likely.

We must accept, first of all, that God has limited his power by 'withdrawing' from the world. Not 'opting out' or abandoning us. He still cares. (And how he cares!) But he's given us space. Space to decide how we do things. We have the free will to let selfishness, chaos and cruelty rule the world. We also have the capability to do the most marvellous things. But if free, intelligent beings like ourselves are to exist, then that limits God's power.

Secondly, God has invented the laws of nature. For example, the law of gravity. Things fall. Things fall on us—if we get in their way. God could catch them—but no. He's made the world the way it is. He doesn't change the rules, and that also limits his power.

▨ Few options

At this point, the unbeliever will perhaps ask, if God is as great as some people say, then surely he could have managed things a bit better. No earthquakes, for example. And no mass murderers.

The answer could just be that God had very few options. Scientists have told us that conditions for the creation of the universe and this planet in particular could have existed only very briefly. If the tiniest detail in the distant, distant past had been different, then the Earth would not have supported life. Indeed, planet Earth might not have 'happened' at all.

Science suggests the whole of creation is a very deli-cate balancing act. The slightest alteration, either at its inception or now, and the balance is lost. Note, too, just how much *we* can unbalance it—for example, by polluting the atmosphere or allowing war to break out.

▨ A delicate balance

Furthermore, it seems almost as if this delicate balance is necessary for religious faith itself to exist.

Were creation that little bit more perfect, we'd have *proof* of the existence of God and then there would be no room for trust or for belief. God's power is far more subtle than anything suggested by the word 'all-powerful' (which is why I prefer the word 'almighty').

Completing creation

It's almost as though God has made a deliberately less-than-perfect world and given us the honour of helping him to put it right, to assist in creation.

In some ways this is a Jewish idea, as Moshe Davis once told me:

> *It is our duty in the world to continue to complete creation. This is a Jewish concept. Man is a partner with God in the works of creation—so we did not find the world in a state of completion. This is a world where there are still deficiencies. For example, there is disease. My job is to see what I can do to discover medicines which will remove it. We believe that it is our task to find the means to improve the world. This is part of the ongoing process of creation.*

It is an idea from which the Christian can usefully learn. Yes, I know that it is almost cheeky to suggest that we dare to think of ourselves as partners with God, but I'm sure that is what he wishes. Sometimes our contributions (in the shape of new discoveries and inventions) prove disastrous and even destructive. But our actions can also be truly creative and beneficial.

A friend of mine, a doctor who treats cancer patients, once told me how depressed he gets when he sees lungs and throats that have suffered the effects of heavy smoking. Two things can always cheer him up, however. One is seeing a patient who has conquered the smoking habit and is slowly making progress to a healthy life. The other is reading about a new piece of successful medical research in *The Lancet*.

▦ Ongoing creation

It is wrong, I think, to imagine God making the world once and for all in some distant era, and thinking, 'Right, that's that done. Needn't do any more to that.' Nor, later on, did he decide it had got into a bit of a mess and send his Son to sort it out, believing it would then be all right for another few thousand years.

No. Creation is constantly developing and changing—and not just through human intervention.

God didn't, for example, make the first two horses and leave them to get on with it. The horse has developed over the centuries.

And for some reason, God made huge, giant, wondrous dinosaurs. But by some means or other they were removed before we came along. For the believer, that may mean that God was developing or perhaps improving his earlier work.

But in humankind, amazingly, God has made creatures that can help him in this development. For example, in 1955 and in 1961, two vaccines (the Salk and Sabin vaccines) were introduced which have nearly removed the once terrifying disease of polio from the world. Just as the discovery and development of vaccination defeated smallpox, they have also almost defeated polio and are on the way to defeating measles. Whether those involved in these advances believe in God or not, they are still his partners in the ongoing creation of the world.

Plenty to do

If the world is going to be a better place for our existence in it, we've all got to care about the rest of the world—not just for what we'll get out of it but because we must be ready to sacrifice a little time for the needs of others. This commitment means more than nodding sympathetically after a television documentary about down-and-outs, or sending money to a charity. That's part of it, but commitment is also about being prepared to put ourselves out to help someone else. It's going out of our way to help the invalid; it's being an audience for the tedious old bore who always tells the same long-winded story. It's remembering that, despite the haste and bustle of modern living, life is nothing if we do not care for those who are near us.

As the poet John Donne once wrote,

No man is an island, entire of itself; every man is a piece of the continent, a part of the main… Any man's death diminishes me, because I am involved in Mankind; and therefore never send to know for whom the bell tolls, it tolls for thee.

So by involving ourselves in the needs of others, we are participating in creation—and helping to reduce the amount of suffering in the world.

For some, it means helping at a domestic, local level. For others, as I said earlier, it can mean using skills in medicine. Equally, it could be skills in education, the arts, engineering, design, law, and even politics!

Times past

Saying that we are partners in creation, that we must work to remove the causes of suffering, does raise the terrible question: how can all the suffering that has gone on in the past be justified?

If we take the field of medicine again, why did God let people suffer long before there was any chance of modern medicines helping them?

I have to admit I have no answer to this—except to make three points:

◆ In olden times, there were systems of medicine that we have either forgotten or now largely ignore in the West. There is, for example, the traditional Chinese system which has been used for centuries. In Roman and medieval times, much intelligent use was made of herbs and drugs extracted from plants. The past was not a period of total ignorance.

◆ A lot of modern suffering is very recent, caused by our careless or thoughtless use of such discoveries and inventions as Valium, asbestos and the motor car. Some suffering is also caused by the affluence that those of us in the West now enjoy—wealth which permits us to indulge in too rich a diet, too much alcohol and too much sun-bathing in climates for which our skin is unsuited.

◆ It is only in recent times that we have begun to think we deserve a long and largely pain-free life. Despite the Book of Psalms in the Bible referring to our natural life as being three score years and ten, life expectancy as recently as 1900 was no more than forty-five years of age in Britain and the rest of the developed world. Less than a hundred years later, it is still only seventy-five years of age.
   I believe this improvement is, incidentally, another example of how we have worked with God in the process of creation.

The modern way of death

There is a further point to consider about the way we view death today. Because most deaths in the West now take place in hospitals and nursing homes, we do not come face to face with death in the way people did in the past. Despite all the violence we see on television, I would guess that many people under the age of fifty have never seen a dead body. Children, in particular, are shielded from the reality of death.

But our present habit of hiding death away only makes it more frightening. By trying to protect ourselves from it, by hiding it away, we actually increase our own distress and suffering when we cannot avoid either death itself or the suffering that surrounds it. As Buddhists remind us, we need to face up to the fact of suffering and our own mortality.

Cultivate the garden

There is a story called *Candide*, written by a Frenchman named Voltaire. It tells of Candide's travels around the world during which he suffers a tempest, a shipwreck, an earthquake, flogging, the loss of his friends, bereavement and much more. At the end of all this, he ends up in a small garden with his friend Pangloss with whom he often enjoys conversation.

'We must go and work in the garden,' said Candide.
'You are quite right,' said Pangloss. 'When man was placed in the Garden of Eden, he was put there ''to dress it and to keep it''—to work,

in fact; which proves that man was not born to an easy life.'

And from time to time, Pangloss says something like this:

'There is a chain of events in this best of all possible worlds; for if you had not suffered all you have suffered, you would not be here eating candied fruit and pistachio nuts.'
'That's true enough,' said Candide; 'but we must go and cultivate the garden.'

We, too, must work with God in whatever 'garden' he has put us in. And by limiting his power, he has made room for us to be his co-workers there.

This, I believe, is one of the great wonders of the world. God could be all-powerful, but only at the price of overthrowing human freedom, and he chooses not to. I also believe that, amazingly frequently, he does intervene simply because we ask him to do so. Which is why he remains 'Almighty God'.

Summing up . . .

God allows us to work with him in the act of creation—and the relief of suffering.

10

Daddy, Daddy, Catch Me!

On different evenings, two men stand on the same spot, staring up at the night sky. Both evenings are cold and frosty. The sky is clear and both see the same stars, bright against the blackness. One man is standing there one night some six hundred years ago; the other is a modern rationalist.

The medieval man is full of wonder, seeing how the stars move at God's command, how they are part of a world in which all things are connected and move in harmony. The moon, the planets—they are all part of God's system, just as he himself is part of a loving God's purposes. He is higher than the animals, lower than the angels. And so far as daily life is concerned—well, it has its ups and downs, but the medieval man still *trusts*.

The modern rationalist is also full of wonder— but it's a different kind of wonder. It's a series of questions about light years and black holes, radio waves and the icy coldness of outer space. And for rationalists, the human race is just another piece of matter that happens to have evolved in this great, accidental, impersonal universe.

The idea that the whole universe is constructed for what used to be called the *summum bonum* or the supreme good is extraordinary to many brought up on the belief that only what we can measure is real.

This is one of the extraordinary features of modern humanity. We know more about the world and the universe, and more about how we ourselves function and behave, than any other generation. But we have real problems when it comes to faith or belief.

Trust me!

Perhaps the real problem is our inability to trust— for belief and trust are not quite the same thing. The little girl, balancing on a wall, cries out, 'Daddy, Daddy, catch me!' She not only *believes* her father will catch her, she also *trusts* her father to catch her.

There is a story told about the French acrobat, Charles Blondin. In 1859, he walked across the Niagara Falls on a tightrope. A little later, he did the same thing but this time pushing a wheelbarrow. A challenge was then issued: 'Do you believe he can do that with a man in the wheelbarrow? 'Yes,' replied all the spectators. 'So then,' came the next challenge, 'do you trust him to do it with you in the wheel-barrow?'

I once heard about a sixteen-year-old boy who eventually learned to swim after years of being terrified of water. At first he would go into the swimming pool and just stand there, not daring to risk taking his feet off the bottom. But because he was an intelligent lad, he finally conquered his fear by going down the steps at the deep end. 'I knew I was safer out of my depth because there was more water to hold me up,' he said.

If you can't swim, it's not easy to take that step of trusting the water to support you. You may have seen plenty of other people floating or swimming. It's different when it's you.

'No' leads nowhere

When it comes to faith in God and belief that he will care for us, it requires a similar act of trust. Many people cannot take this step. 'No. The suffering of Auschwitz and of Rwanda, the suffering of Aberfan and of African famines are too much. I cannot trust.'

But that 'no' leads nowhere.

Saying 'Yes'

There is a kind of acting game that is sometimes played in drama lessons in school. In it you have to say 'yes'. The point of the game is to help students and actors to improvise little scenes. The only rule of the game is that the second line of the dialogue must be 'yes'. If it's not, the improvisation fails—like this:

> SHE: *I say, I gather you speak Russian.*
> HE: *No.*
> SHE: *You don't?*
> HE: *No, not at all.*

End of scene; end of conversation—it's leading nowhere. But suppose the answer is 'yes':

> SHE: *I say, I gather you speak Russian.*
> HE: *Yes, I do actually.*
> SHE: *Where did you learn?*

And that's the start of a scene the two actors can develop at some length. Progress is possible.

Saying 'yes' requires courage. Saying 'yes' to faith requires courage for it means taking things on trust. And, in the end, all our questions about the problem of suffering can be answered only by saying 'yes' to a mystery; by accepting that there are things we do not and will not understand in this life.

Some definite purpose

For twenty years, I walked home each night along the same short path. On winter evenings, I, too, looked up at the slowly wheeling constellations as they made their annual journey across the sky. And on summer evenings, especially after rain, I savoured the scent of stocks and carnations and a flower whose name I never knew which grew there.

It was in those moments, miraculously repeated many times a year, that I came to believe quite firmly that there is a purpose behind all things. In the infinite mathematical precision of the heavens and the subtlety of those transient petals, I found the truth of the words written by the nineteenth-century English Catholic, Cardinal Newman:

> *God has created me to do him some definite purpose. He has committed some work to me which he has not committed to another. I have my mission. I may never know it in this world, but I shall be told of it in the next.*
>
> *I am a link in the chain, a bond of connection between persons. He has not created me for naught... He knows what he is about... He may make me feel desolate, make my spirits sink, hide my future from me... Still, he knows what he is about.*

▩ Hold fast

It can be hard to hold fast to that belief, hard to carry on trusting when we feel really desolate or when our spirits sink at the thought of all the suffering of the world. And it can be hard to trust when God seems distant, or when his ways seem strange.

On the morning of the Aberfan disaster, there had been fog. One school bus, bringing children from an outlying village, had been delayed. Those children had not reached the school when the disaster happened and so were safe. Now did God intervene that morning by sending fog? And if he saved those children, why not the others? Was he perhaps limited by our actions, our carelessness? The only answer is: 'We don't know. It's a mystery.'

Whatever you ask

But an even greater mystery and wonder is that we can help God to intervene—by our prayers and our action. Jesus said, 'Whatever you ask in prayer, you will receive if you have faith.' This does not mean we are going to get an instantaneous 'yes' to every request we put to God. Although he is almighty, he is not a neighbourhood chemist with an overnight cure for every ill. He doesn't hand out free £10 notes to suit our idle whim, nor does he make the sun shine just because we're on holiday and no one else is. Like the good father that he is, he knows what's best for us—and what is possible.

Some Christians who are ill go on pilgrimage to Lourdes in France, or to the English shrine of Walsingham in Norfolk, in the hope that they will be cured when they get there. Some are physically cured. Some aren't. So are some people's prayers better than others? I doubt it works that way.

On the other hand, if we say God *can't* intervene at our request, there is no point in praying. What we have to accept is that the answer to our prayer may not be immediate or obvious—or that what we're asking is impossible, given the free will of other people and the natural laws of the universe.

Intervention?

Yet God does sometimes seem to intervene in an immediate and obvious way. Take an incident that happened to me in the small hours of the morning of 1 June 1992. I was woken out of a deep sleep by a noise which seemed like a branch of a tree hitting my bedroom window.

Being woken up at that moment allowed me to reach my mother's bedside and speak to her just before she died. Now was that coincidence, or intervention?

Faith, hope and charity

God's priority seems to be to bring us to a position where we have trust, hope and love—or 'faith, hope and charity', to use the words of Paul in the Bible.

To achieve this, God doesn't seduce us by displays of magic. In fact, he almost always hides his actions so that there is always room for doubt as well as faith (for faith cannot exist without there being room for doubt). As my vicar once said, 'If we knew for certain just how glorious heaven will be, we'd be tempted to go there prematurely.'

So there must be an element of doubt and uncertainty; an element of mystery. This can be the only conclusion to our search for an answer to the question as to why there should be unjustified suffering in the world. It *can't* be explained. It *is* a mystery which the human mind cannot solve. We cannot properly understand a creation in which a vixen cares for her fox cubs with all her being and is a wonderful example of dedicated motherhood—and then goes off and kills more chickens than she and they can eat.

Nor can we understand why human beings who are sometimes so wonderful can also do such terrible things. Take one moment in Shakespeare's play *Hamlet*. Prince Hamlet is in the deepest despair, overcome with profound gloom. He's learned that his father was murdered, his mother has hastily married his uncle and, as he's just been told, it was his uncle who murdered his father. In his deep, deep despair he begins to think of suicide.

The earth, the sky, the heavens, the people around him seem to hold no attraction for him. And yet ... Even in his suffering and mental agony, he can still see what is wondrous about a human being, and about our mental and physical capabilities.

What a piece of work is a man, how noble in reason, how infinite in faculties, in form and moving, how express and admirable in action, how like an angel in apprehension, how like a god: the beauty of the world; the paragon of animals.

It may be hard to hold to this belief on days when the news is full of stories about our cruelty and thoughtlessness, about child abuse and terrorist attacks. But as Shakespeare points out when Hamlet uses the word 'paragon', we can come close to perfection—close, even, to being like the angels. We can become God's co-workers for a better world, overcoming suffering with good.

Accepting the mystery

So the best we can say is that we must accept the mystery. This, essentially, is the heart of the Christian faith. Although we human beings have to face up to coping with life, including the problem of suffering, one basic support is clear. God is saying to us, 'Yes, you may have to go through all this suffering and pain but you don't have to do it on your own. Through Jesus Christ, who suffered on the cross, I am in the middle of it all with you.'

Footprints

The whole message of the New Testament is that God actually shares in the human life and in the human condition—and I wouldn't be a Christian if I didn't believe that God isn't in the midst of human suffering. The fact that he may not always appear to be here can be explained by this well-known parable.

As a Christian lay dying, he saw his life stretched out across the sands of time. For most of his life there were two sets of footprints and he knew that one of them were his own and the other set belonged to the Lord Jesus. But then he noticed that, at certain points, there was only one set of footprints. He noticed that this had happened at the saddest moments in his life.

This puzzled him, so when he met the Lord Jesus he asked him, 'Lord, I don't understand. Why was it, when I needed you most, that there was only one set of footprints? Why did you leave me?'

And the Lord Jesus replied, 'My precious son, I love you and I would never leave you. During those times of suffering when you see only one set of footprints, it was then that I was carrying you.'

No slick answers

Like the little girl on the wall, we can trust our Father in heaven to catch us. We can trust that he *is* a loving God, that he does not want us to suffer, but wants us to make positive use of the fact that the world is made in such a way that suffering has to happen.

I think that part of growing up is being able to accept the mysterious elements in human life: accepting that, despite all our advances, there are many things to which we just don't know the answers; accepting, too, that slick answers to big questions are nearly always wrong answers. There simply isn't a neat, tidy solution. What there is, however, is assurance; assurance that God is in the world supporting each one of us. Like the person in the story of the footprints, we may not always feel it. That doesn't make it less true.

▨ All shall be well

I don't find the problem of suffering destroys my faith. In practice, my faith helps me to make sense of life. As the great saint, Augustine, put it, *Credo ut intelligam* (I believe in order that I may understand). This is not the same as saying that faith makes life softer.

But with faith we can become aware of the mystery of life. Whatever we suffer, God is with us, calling us to a further stage in our life's journey.

Sometimes we will feel lonely. Sometimes we will sense he is very near. What we can rely on, I can only repeat, is the assurance that he *is* supporting us— and, provided we trust him, he will not let us drown.

What we have to do is accept a truth stated by Mother Julian of Norwich back in the fifteenth century when she wrote about the teachings of Jesus:

He said not, 'Thou shalt not be tempested, thou shalt not be travailed, thou shalt not be afflicted, but he said, 'thou shalt not be overcome...'.

And, as she said in another place,

And all shall be well, and all manner of thing shall be well.

Like the boy learning to swim, we've got to risk getting into deep water—but once we do jump in at the deep end, we'll find it isn't a leap into the dark, but a leap into the light.

▓ Summing up . . .

1   A lot of suffering is our own deliberate fault.

2   A lot of suffering is the result of our carelessness.

3   A lot of suffering *doesn't* seem to be our fault but—

4   A world without suffering would mean we did not have free will.

5   Several religions teach us either simply to accept suffering, or that it is a punishment, or a test of our faith.

6   But the fact that seemingly good people suffer remains a real problem.

7   However, God has shared and does share in our suffering.

8   Although the suffering of the world is neither a
    test nor a punishment, it does allow us to use our
    intelligence to improve the world and to be caring,
    self-sacrificing and helpful to those in distress.

9   God has created all things for the best but has left
    room for us to co-operate with him in the
    perfection of creation.

10 There is no easy answer to the problem of
    unjustified suffering. It must remain a mystery, but
    we have God's assurance that, if we trust him, he
    will not fail us. In the end, all shall be well.

Index

Also from Lion Publishing:

CLIMBING OUT OF DEPRESSION

Sue Atkinson

Depression is a dark and isolating experience.
Countless people suffer from it.

Anyone who has fallen into a pit of depression
wants to climb back out. But that is not easy to do.
Depressed people often feel paralyzed into inaction.

So help is needed—practical, humane and spiritual
help—which is just what this book offers.

Sue Atkinson has suffered years of depression
herself. She does not write as an expert on depression,
or a depression counsellor, but as someone who knows
the feelings from close personal experience.

This is a book to dip into as fits a person's mood and
the need of the moment. The reader will find it a
dependable guide for the climb.

ISBN 0 7459 2248 1

UNDERSTANDING PANIC ATTACKS AND OVERCOMING FEAR

Dr Roger Baker

At least one and a half million people in Britain alone suffer from panic attacks. And yet panic attacks are little understood by the public at large, and are not infrequently misdiagnosed by the medical profession.

This book

◆ explains what a panic attack is

◆ dispels the myths about panic

◆ sets up practical measures to overcome fear and panic.

In clear and concise language Dr Baker enables sufferers to start on the road to recovery. It is a book that will also be of enormous benefit to the family and friends of sufferers, making understanding the key to recovery.

ISBN 0 7459 3313 0